Rose
Elliot's
Complete
Vegan

First published in the UK and USA in 2019 by Nourish,
an imprint of Watkins Media Limited
Unit 11 Shepperton House
83–93 Shepperton Road
London, N1 3DF
enquiries@nourishbooks.com

Publisher: Jo Lal
Managing Editor: Daniel Hurst
Head of Design: Georgina Hewitt
Copyeditor: Emily Preece-Morrison
Photography: Kim Lightbody
Food Stylist: Valerie Berry
Prop Stylist: Rachel Vere

Typeset in Walbaum and Cera Pro
Colour reproduction by XY Digital
Printed in China
A CIP record for this book is available from the British Library

ISBN: 978-1-84899-375-4

10 9 8 7 6 5 4 3 2 1

Publisher's note
While every care has been taken in compiling the recipes for this
book, Watkins Media Limited, or any other persons who have been
involved in working on this publication, cannot accept responsibility
for any errors or omissions, inadvertent or not, that may be found in
the recipes or text, nor for any problems that may arise as a result of
preparing one of these recipes. If you are pregnant or breastfeeding
or have any special dietary requirements or medical conditions, it is
advisable to consult a medical professional before following any of
the recipes contained in this book.

Notes on the recipes
Unless otherwise stated:
Use medium fruit and vegetables
Use medium (US large) organic or free-range eggs
Use fresh herbs, spices and chillies
Use granulated sugar (Americans can use ordinary granulated sugar
when caster sugar is specified)
Do not mix metric, imperial and US cup measurements:
1 tsp = 5ml 1 tbsp = 15ml 1 cup = 240ml

nourishbooks.com

*To vegans and would-be
vegans everywhere: our
time has come. Let's 'be
the change we wish to
see' – and celebrate!*

Rose Elliot's Complete Vegan

NOURISH

EAT WELL, LIVE WELL

contents

introduction

Welcome! Whether you've been vegan – or eating a plant-based diet – for some time, or are just putting a toe in the water now, this is the book for you. Within its pages, you'll find the answers to your questions, something delicious to eat and all the tools you need to live a vegan lifestyle with ease.

Personally, I was brought up as a vegetarian and have never eaten meat in my life, and gradually, over time I also stopped eating any dairy produce until my diet became completely vegan, which it has been for a number of years now. In fact, my three daughters and two of my granddaughters are now vegan too; it seems a natural progression for many vegetarians. Recent years have seen the vegan movement go from strength to strength and many people are now turning to plant-based lifestyles for ethical, environmental and health reasons. Because of this the breadth and quality of vegan products readily available has greatly increased and there has never been a better time to be vegan! It is a wonderful way to live and eat and I thoroughly recommend it.

There are an abundance of resources all over the internet and different recipes and advice, but I wanted to write this book to bring all the basics together in one place as a 'go to' vegan reference book, as well as offering some showstoppers ... I wanted to take the same approach as I had always done for my vegetarian cookery books – offering timeless family favourites, simple stunning suppers, meals for every occasion, in fact, together with lots of practical tips and ideas that I have found helpful in my own cooking.

what 'going vegan' means in practice?

Depending on what your starting point is, going vegan can be a gradual process or something that happens overnight, and everyone's personal experience is unique. Making the change can be straightforward if you're already vegetarian – many vegetarians find, as I did, that over time they naturally become more and more vegan in their eating and lifestyle – but there are equally some who feel quite dependent on cheese as a flavour and ingredient and find it hard to imagine cutting it out completely. There are also countless people making the change from a 'traditional' meat-eating diet straight to veganism. It may feel quite different at the beginning: looking carefully at ingredients lists when shopping (see p.16–17), telling friends about your dietary needs when they cook for you, and asking for a special menu when you eat out. Whatever your starting point, if you feel the urge to 'go vegan', I encourage you to give it a try.

A good way to make the changes and to ensure they stick can be to introduce some simple swaps to your usual diet: change from dairy milk to plant milk, eat veggie burgers instead of beef burgers, vegan cheese instead of dairy; or perhaps make one meal a week, or even one meal a day, completely plant-based, if you think you can do it: breakfast or lunch are good ones to pick, and then you might like to treat yourself to a good vegan meal in a restaurant, vegan fast food place, or whatever takes your fancy. There are many options, we're getting spoilt for choice, unlike when I was growing up as a vegetarian and all we could get was a choice of an omelette or a simple salad!

Some people will decide to dive straight in and become vegan overnight, and with all the information and products now available it's easier than ever to take the plunge. It's a personal thing, and only you can know what will work for you. In my experience, 'going vegan' is a journey, so take it at your own pace, and don't give up or worry too much at any setbacks along the way. If you make the intention to succeed, you'll get there in the end – and every little change you make helps you on your way.

One thing I can say is that most people are amazed and delighted at how delicious vegan food is, and also at how easy it can be to make. Indeed, it can be as elaborate and 'gourmet', or as simple and budget-priced, as you like; the choice is yours. You will find many recipes and ideas for snacks and meals for all occasions in this book and I hope you will enjoy them.

being a healthy vegan

The healthiness of the diet is endorsed by many authorities internationally; you can read what they say online, but here's just one of them from the Academy of Nutrition and Dietetics, 2016:

'*Appropriately planned vegetarian including vegan, diets are healthful, nutritionally adequate, and may provide health benefits for the prevention and treatment of certain diseases. These diets are appropriate for all stages of the life cycle, including pregnancy, lactation, infancy, childhood, adolescence, older adulthood, and for athletes. Plant based diets are more environmentally sustainable than diets rich in animal products because they use fewer natural resources and are associated with much less environmental damage.*'

And Dr Mark Porter, writing recently as *the Times* doctor, stated that '*Vegans, like vegetarians, tend to have healthier cholesterol profiles and lower blood pressure, suffer fewer early heart attacks and strokes, are less likely to develop diabetes and appear to be at lower risk of developing some types of common cancer, such as bowel and prostate.*'

There are excellent vegan sources for all the essential nutrients as you can see on p.18–19 and for extra protection, if you wish, you can always take a specially balanced vegan vitamin to put your mind at rest.

Having said that, I must admit that there is such a thing as an unhealthy vegan and people who describe themselves as 'junk food vegans', but I don't recommend that approach. However, if you base your diet on plants and eat food as close to its natural state as possible, it is a remarkably healthy lifestyle.

extending the circle of compassion

Because what we eat has a huge impact on us and our view of life and the environment in which we live, once you start the vegan journey, you may find you begin to look at many things in a different way; you'll most likely feel your 'circle of compassion' extending to other aspects of your life as well as food. This includes personal clothes and products – you may not wish to wear leather, wool, fur or feathers, for instance, or to use make-up or cleaning materials that include animal products or, certainly, that have been tested on animals.

This can affect our choice of soap, cosmetics, cleaning products, paint and household materials, and even entertainments that can be said to exploit animals such as circuses, zoos ... How far you want to go is a personal matter, following your own conscience and inner feelings, but in my experience the more you practise the vegan way of life, the wider your circle of compassion extends. In fact, recent studies suggest that switching to a vegan diet can be the biggest way to reduce our environmental impact on earth.

Researchers at the University of Oxford found that cutting meat and dairy products from their diet could reduce a person's carbon footprint from food by up to 73 per cent, helping protect our land, ecosystems, oceans, rivers, seas and air: reducing greenhouse gas emissions and climate change, and, yes, truly making it possible to feed the world.

So veganism really does become a way of life, and is challenging in some respects, but exciting and rewarding too. You can take it step by step, at your own pace, as I have done over the years, doing your best to eat and live in a way that is consistent with your conscience and a compassionate way of life. People may be combative because veganism challenges their accepted beliefs about food, agriculture, the treatment of animals, and lifestyle; and they fear change, but the benefits of the diet both personally, ecologically, and globally, are so great that the arguments are overwhelming.

I believe that a vegan diet is best for us, best for the animals and best for the environment. The vegan lifestyle brings new opportunities – the need for alternative solutions leads to inventiveness, finding new ways of doing things, new friendships and alliances; so it can be very heart-warming and exciting too. And everyone agrees that the food, which can be as simple or exotic as you like, is delicious! So come on in, and join the party!

Rose

my journey to veganism

One of my earliest memories is of watching my mother preparing herrings for supper and realising that they were dead. I asked her whether they had been killed specially for us to eat, and I can still remember the shock that ran through me when she replied that they had. As it happened, she and my father were practically vegetarian; they had given up red meat some time ago, but still ate fish and chicken occasionally. I think my outburst that night hastened their transition to being complete vegetarian, which wasn't particularly easy in those days (the early 1950s). My younger sister and I were the only vegetarians at our primary school; vegetarian lunches could not be provided, and our wholemeal salad sandwiches, carrot sticks and salad leaves, nuts and raisins, and bottles of fresh juice were objects of stunned amazement to the rest of the school. It was difficult at first, but we got used to it, and I really admire my mother for being a pioneer of healthy and compassionate eating.

I followed her lead and remember sending to the Vegan Society for information and my sister and I trying to make vegan milk from whole soya beans in our little kitchen at home when I was about 12 years old. It involved soaking, boiling and sieving (no liquidizers or food processors then), and I think we used every saucepan available. My sister who was tackling the mountains of washing up I had created, remembers to this day how, with the kitchen piled high with used bowls, sieves, saucepans, jugs, and every other piece of equipment you can imagine, I said brightly 'now let's try making vegan butter' ...

Being vegan – even, let's face it, being vegetarian – was so difficult in those days. But the desire never left me. I was 'practically vegan', giving up eggs and dairy produce; and then reverting back to being vegetarian, for a long time. Over the years however my vegan times became longer and longer; I wrote two vegan cookbooks, *The Green Age Diet*, and *Vegan Feasts*, and included vegan variations and alternatives in my vegetarian cookbooks. I have been wanting to write a more comprehensive vegan cook book for some time, so I was thrilled when Nourish approached me with the possibility writing this book: *Rose Elliot's Complete Vegan*. It's the result of years of vegetarian/vegan cookery writing which started in response to the many requests I had for the recipes for the dishes that I cooked up for the visitors to the retreat centre where I worked from the age of 16.

Writing this book has been such a joy; the enthusiasm everyone has expressed for knowing more about the vegan diet and way of life; and for trying the food; the challenge of 'veganizing' some of my most popular vegetarian recipes from the past, and of creating new and original recipes that are vegan in their own right. I have loved seeing the mixture of pleasure and amazement on the faces of those who have tasted my inventions. And I have been so grateful as well to those dear friends and family who have been kind enough to share their own favourite recipes and inventions with me for this book: in particular, my three daughters, who have travelled the vegan journey with me, and given me for this book some wonderful recipes that they have created.

Although I was vegetarian from birth, it was some years before I became completely vegan. During that time, public awareness of the effect of our food choices upon the planet, wildlife, the rain forests and indeed our own health have become more and more evident. I truly love making, eating (and writing about!) vegan food, but it also gives me great satisfaction to know that in doing so I can, and I am, helping to protect the wildlife, the animals, and the whole ecology of this beautiful planet. As Joseph Poore at the University of Oxford, said: *'a vegan diet is probably the single biggest way to reduce your impact on planet Earth, not just greenhouse gasses, but global acidification, eutrophication, land use and water use.'* The foods we choose to cook and eat truly can change the world.

the vegan storecupboard

It's a wonderful time to go vegan; the range of foods and ingredients in shops, supermarkets, and online has never been greater. There are great vegan versions of many dairy and meat products and they are increasing and improving all the time. So, I say, if you feel drawn to the vegan way of life, just get started! It gets easier and more natural all the time and by choosing to buy and cook vegan you are not only enjoying great food, but are also making a huge difference to the welfare of animals, your own health, the state of the planet ...

Many food products state if they are vegan. I usually check the list of ingredients: the shorter this is, and the more natural the items on it, the better. If you're unsure you can always look online and refer to the handy guide on p.16–17 for the most common ingredients to avoid. I like to buy organic, too, whenever I can. And, for reasons I have described on p.8, I do my absolute best to avoid products (food, cleaners, personal care and make up) containing palm oil, including 'sustainable' palm oil. You may have to look it up under some of the different creative names that manufacturers use for it.

When following a vegan diet there are some ingredients that will be mainstays of the food that you make and form part of any well-stocked vegan pantry. Here are the most useful ingredients to have in stock:

plant milks

There are many to choose from, with different flavours and textures, some thicker than others, some sweetened, some not. I prefer unsweetened for everything (you can always add but not take away!) and for everyday use on cereals, in drinks, and for most cooking I like KoKo, which is quite a 'thin' milk, but for making mayonnaise and vegan double cream I use a thicker one such as oat or soy, though I try not to over-use the latter, simply because soy creeps into so many manufactured foods. Vegan yogurt and single cream are also available: I like a plain unflavoured supermarket brand of yogurt which I've also successfully used as a 'starter' for making my own yogurt (see p.24). Coconut Milk, available in cans everywhere, is very useful: keep a couple of cans in the fridge so that it separates, then pour off the liquid and use the rest as cream in sweet and savoury recipes. You can make your own plant milks using the recipes on p.266.

oils and fats

KTC solid white coconut oil, which is unflavoured, and useful for many recipes, including for making the most delicious vegan butter (see p.266). Light olive oil is also useful for other recipes, including mayonnaise (p.258); also, for deep-frying, dark olive oil; avocado oil is expensive but health-giving to use for cooking; I occasionally use organic rapeseed oil for frying.

canned and jarred beans and vegetables

I use chickpeas the most, partly because I love them, but also because the water they're canned in, *'aquafaba' or* 'bean water', when chilled, can be whisked like egg white to make meringues (see p.244) (The same applies to the water from other beans, but I prefer the delicate colour and flavour of chickpea water. Cans of tomatoes are also useful, and jars of artichoke hearts in oil.

nuts and seeds

There are many availablle and I like to use a variety: Walnuts, pine nuts, plain and roasted cashews, almonds, pecans, hazelnuts, brazils, ground almonds, sesame seeds, sunflower seeds, pumpkin seeds, flax seeds, chia seeds, sesame seeds and hemp seeds.

vegan protein foods

I use the traditional ones made from natural proteins: tofu, made from soya beans, and seitan, from wheat gluten. Tofu can be delicate 'silken', medium firm, firm, extra firm, marinated, or smoked. They all have their uses in different recipes. You don't need a tofu press, you can simply buy the firm or extra firm varieties. Wheat protein, or seitan, has a chewy texture. Follow the manufacturer's directions for cooking, or buy it already prepared: I like a canned one by granovita which is somewhat unfortunately named 'Mock Duck'.

sweeteners

Maple syrup, golden syrup and black treacle all give sweetness and flavour. Believe it or not, some sugars are not vegan because bone char is used in the manufacturing process, so you need to check brands of both brown and white sugar online: look for the phrases beet, unrefined, USDA, organic, and raw. Molasses, demerara (turbinado), and muscovado sugar are never filtered through bone char.

nutritional yeast flakes

These are very useful for adding a nutty, cheesy flavour and a rich source of protein, fibre and folic acid. I love them.

flours

Plain (all-purpose) and self-raising white flour; wholemeal (whole wheat) for some recipes, also cornflour (corn starch), chickpea (gram) flour and tapioca flour.

sea vegetables

Nori Seaweed, for wrapping sushi and making 'Tofish' (see p.126); wakame for crumbling into a big mug, adding boiling water and a spoonful of delicious brown rice miso for this cook's favourite pick-me-up drink!

flavourings, herbs and spices

For quick and easy stock I like Marigold vegetable bouillon powder – the vegan one with salt; miso paste, pale and dark; shoyu-style soy sauce and tamari, a Japanese version of shoyu with little or no gluten; tomato purée (paste); ready-made vegan mustard; cider vinegar; red wine vinegar; rice vinegar; tabasco sauce; salt – I prefer Celtic sea salt or pink Himalayan salt – I also use *Kala Namak* or 'black' salt, which has a sulphurous taste and odour reminiscent of eggs, making the perfect addition to vegan omelettes or scrambles; freshly ground black pepper; garlic powder/granules; onion powder/granules; whole and ground cumin; smoked and normal paprika; cayenne pepper; ground turmeric; ground cinnamon; mixed spice; black pepper; liquid smoke; chilli powder; saffron (occasionally); mustard powder; dried mixed herbs or *herbes de Provence*; dried red chillies; fresh root ginger; garam masala; ground coriander; black or brown mustard seeds; cardamom pods; cinnamon sticks.

pasta

There is an excellent range of egg-free pastas in all shapes and sizes available in the free-from section of all good supermarkets.

egg replacer

Cooking without eggs is easier than everyone thinks. You can use various mixtures to replicate the texture that eggs give to baked goods, such as ground flax seeds and water to give the binding consistency of eggs, but I don't find these necessary. I do however user an 'egg replacer' – Orgram – in my recipe for Yorkshire puddings (p.176), which turn out beautifully. Otherwise I simply use self-raising flour with extra baking powder, bicarbonate of soda (baking soda), and one of the thicker plant milks, eg soy, almond, or oat milk soured with lemon juice; just follow the recipes: you'll be amazed.

food labels explained

Many foods that may seem vegan on the surface can contain hidden animal ingredients, so it is important to always check food labels thoroughly for hidden nasties. Below is a list of the most commonly found ingredients to avoid:

- **Albumen** – the white of an egg (see below)
- **Aspic** – similar to gelatine (see below). Made from clarified meat stock.
- **Casein** – a form of milk protein.
- **Cod liver oils** – found in beauty products and taken in tablet form as a supplement.
- **Collagen** – derived from the skin, bones and connective tissues of livestock.
- **Eggs** – the unfertilised embryo of an animal (in food production, usually chicken).
- **Elastin** – derived from the aorta and ligaments of bovine animals.
- **Gelatine** – derived by boiling the skin, bones, tendons and ligaments of cows and pigs.
- **Honey** – the natural energy source produced by bees.
- **Isinglass** – used in the clarification of some wines and beers. Derived from fish swim bladders.
- **Keratin** – derived from the skin, bones and connective tissues of livestock.
- **Lactose** – a milk sugar.
- **Lard** – animal fat.
- **Milk (powder), butter, buttermilk**
- **Pepsin** – a clotting agent used in vitamins. Derived from the stomachs of pigs.
- **Propolis** – produced by honey bees when constructing their hives.
- **Royal Jelly** – a honey bee secretion used to nourish larvae.
- **Shellac** – a resin secreted by female scale insects. Used in food and beauty products.
- **Vitamin D3** – derived from sheep's wool or fish liver oil.
- **Whey** – a by-product of milk production.

e-numbers

- **E120** – Carmine or cochineal. Derived from the crushed up bodies of beetles and used as red food colouring.
- **E441** – gelatine (see above).
- **E542** – bone phosphate. Used to keep food moist.
- **E901** – beeswax. Used as a glazing agent.
- **E904** – shellac (see above).
- **E910, E920, E921** – L-cysteine. Made from animal feathers and fur and used in the proving of some breads.
- **E913** – Lanolin. A greasy secretion derived from woolly mammals, such as sheep. Used in cosmetics and the production of Vitamin D3 (see above).
- **E966** – Lactitol. Derived from lactose (see above) and used a sweetener in some foods.

building a healthy vegan diet

Being vegan is not only better for the planet, with a little planning it can also lead to a healthier you. To ensure that your body is getting everything it needs, make sure that your daily food intake includes a good mix of the food types listed below.

fruit and vegetables

Try to consume at least five portions of fruit and veg a day – though some guidelines now recommend ten portions. Make sure that the bulk of your intake comes from vegetables and that you include a good mix covering everything from leafy greens to sweet berries.

iodine

A good source of iodine in your diet helps your body maintain a healthy metabolism. Snack on a couple of sheets of dried seaweed, such as nori, or take it in supplement form.

calcium-rich foods

Hand-in-hand with vitamin D, calcium is essential for strong bones and teeth. Vegan milks and yogurts are good sources.

high-fibre carbohydrates

Foods that are high in fibre are essential for good digestive health and have also been linked to maintaining a healthy weight, lowering the chances of diabetes and as a preventative for heart disease and some forms of cancer. Wholewheat pasta, brown rice, wholemeal bread, oats and starchy vegetables such as sweet potato are all good sources.

selenium-rich foods

Selenium is an important mineral that plays a vital role in boosting the immune system. A couple of Brazil nuts or a cup of cooked brown rice will give you the amount you need. It is also available in supplement form.

vitamin D

Vitamin D is vital for healthy bones, teeth and muscles. In the summer months we can get everything we need from the sunlight, but during autumn (fall) and winter it can be beneficial to take a supplement.

omega-3 fatty acids

Omega-3 fatty acids are essential nutrients that can be instrumental in preventing heart disease and have been linked to lowered blood pressure and slowing the development of plaque in the arteries. Good sources are walnuts, ground flaxseed (linseed) chai seeds and hemp seeds.

vitamin B12

This essential vitamin helps boost memory, mood and concentration. It is also taken as a preventative to Alzheimer's disease. It is found in fortified breakfast cereals, vegan milks and yogurts, nutritional yeast flakes and dairy-free spreads.

a good source of protein

Protein helps to form your body's building blocks, enabling it to repair damaged or diseased cells. Legumes, such as a beans, peas and lentils, soya products and nuts and seeds are all good sources.

iron-rich foods

Iron is essential for helping transport oxygen throughout our bodies. Good sources are legumes, such as peas, beans and lentils; tofu and other soya products; whole grains, nuts and seeds, leafy green vegetables and dried fruit, such as figs, apricots and raisins.

breakfast and brunch

mango
and lime
smoothie

This is a beautiful, simple smoothie to make when you have a really ripe mango. It doesn't need any extra thickening ingredient and tastes wonderful with the sharpness of the lime.

Serves 1

1 ripe mango
1 lime
a little water or ice (optional)

Slice the mango down each side of the stone to obtain 3 sections, one of which contains the stone. This makes it easier to pare away the skin and the stone to obtain the mango flesh. Put all the pieces of mango into a blender. Grate in a little lime zest, if you like, and process until smooth.

Add lime juice to taste and adjust the thickness of the smoothie with a little water or ice, if you like.

banana,
berry and
almond
smoothie

Frozen banana pieces, which you prepare ahead, make a delicious basis for smoothies, being both creamy and thick. I particularly like adding some white almond butter for richness, along with any other fruit that I fancy: strawberries, raspberries and blueberries are all delicious.

Serves 1–2

1 banana, peeled and cut into 2.5cm
    (1in) pieces and frozen until required
1 heaped tsp white almond butter
small handful of your chosen berries
a little water or freshly-squeezed
    orange juice (optional)
a little maple syrup, to taste (optional)

Simply put the frozen banana pieces into a blender, along with the almond butter and berries, and process, adding a little water or juice as necessary to achieve your preferred thickness. Mix in maple syrup, to taste, and serve immediately.

green smoothie

Put the avocado, lettuce, baby leaves and mint into a blender with half of the water and process until smooth. Add the remaining water as required and blend to achieve your preferred thickness. Stir in a little lemon juice and sugar or maple syrup, to taste.

The avocado gives this smoothie a lovely creamy texture and also makes it a sustaining start to the day.

Serves 1

½ avocado, peeled and roughly
    chopped
1 little gem lettuce, roughly chopped
handful of baby leaves, such as rocket
    (arugula) or spinach
1 fresh mint sprig
up to 250ml (9fl oz/1 cup) water
squeeze of lemon juice
dash of sugar or maple syrup, to taste
    (optional)

BREAKFAST BOWLS

Easy to put together, quick and comforting to eat, and infinitely variable, breakfast bowls – or 'breakfast-in-a-bowl' – are both practical and delicious, from hot, Quick Creamy Porridge (p.32), Overnight Oats (p.26) or Homemade Crunchy Granola (p.29), to Summer Berry Compote (p.25) or creamy Homemade Vegan Yogurt (opposite page).

topping suggestions:

- a spoonful of summer berry compôte/or dried fruit compôte (opposite page)
- a swirl of maple syrup and toasted flaked nuts
- Crunchy Granola (p.29)
- a sprinkling of a sweet spice, such as ground cinnamon
- chopped crystallized ginger
- chopped dried fruits
- sliced banana and a spoonful of crunchy brown sugar
- fresh blueberries, strawberries or raspberries

homemade yogurt

This is easy to make using your favourite plant milk (soya milk, or a thicker variety, such as almond or oat milk work best) and a plain (unsweetened) live soya yogurt for the starter. You will also need one or two glass jars with lids. Use a yogurt maker or incubator, if you have one, or have ready two thick, warm towels to wrap your jars in.

Of course, you can buy vegan yogurt. As with all store-bought ready-made foods, I suggest that you always choose a type with the simplest and purest 'real food' ingredients, not something that sounds as though it was invented in a test tube.

Serves 4

For the yogurt (makes 500ml/17fl oz/2 cups):
500ml (17fl oz/2 cups) plant milk of your choice
2 tbsp plain unsweetened live soya yogurt

Sterilize one or two glass jars large enough to hold the quantity of yogurt, and their lids, either in the dishwasher or by filling them completely with boiling water. Leave for a minute or two before tipping it away.

Heat the plant milk for 1 minute on high in the microwave, or bring it to the boil in a saucepan. Allow it to cool to body temperature (so you can't feel it when you place your finger in it).

Whisk the yogurt into the milk, then pour the mixture into your jar or jars and wrap them up snugly in the towels. Leave in a warm place for 14–16 hours until the yogurt has set. After this time, transfer to the refrigerator, where the yogurt will thicken further. It will keep for 5–7 days.

Serve your lovely thick, creamy vegan yogurt with toppings of your choice.

summer berry compôte

Melt the vegan butter in a saucepan over a medium heat, then add the brown sugar and lemon juice. When the sugar has dissolved, add the berries and stir gently to coat them with the sugar mixture. Cook gently for 2–3 minutes until they are warmed through and tender and the juices have started to run.

Let cool before serving.

This looks and tastes beautiful. It's gorgeous for breakfast just as it is, or with yogurt, and also makes a wonderful sauce for pancakes.

Serves 4–6

40g (1½oz/3 tbsp) unsalted Vegan Butter (see p.266)
50g (2oz/¼ cup) soft brown sugar, or to taste
2 tbsp freshly squeezed lemon juice
400g (14oz) mixed summer berries (raspberries, strawberries, blackberries, blueberries)

dried fruit compôte

Put all the ingredients into a medium saucepan, cover with water and leave to soak for 2–3 hours.

Set the pan over a low-medium heat and simmer the mixture, uncovered, for about 30 minutes, until the fruit is very soft and tender and the water has almost disappeared.

Let cool before serving.

This makes a lovely breakfast or brunch dish served with thick vegan yogurt (opposite page).

Serves 4–6

500g (1lb 2oz) mixed dried fruits (apricots, peaches, pears, sultanas, cherries, apple slices)
2–3 crystallized ginger chunks, chopped
1–2 cinnamon sticks (optional)

overnight oats

Serves 1

50g (2oz/½ cup) rolled (old-fashioned)
    oats
250ml (9fl oz/1 cup) liquid of choice
    (soy, almond or other plant milk,
    or apple or orange juice)
dried fruit of choice (optional)

To serve:
spices: ground cinnamon, mixed spice
flavourings: a dash of vanilla
    or 1–2 drops almond essence
sweeteners: a swirl of maple syrup,
    a spinkling of demerara (turbinado)
    sugar
nuts or seeds, roughly chopped or
    ground: flaked (slivered) almonds,
    walnuts, pecans, or brazils, chia or
    flax seeds
a spoonful of thick creamy vegan
    yogurt
a spoonful of naturally sweetened jam
    (jelly)
a spoonful of nut butter, such as
    almond
fresh or cooked fruit: gently poached
    rhubarb, chopped banana,
    strawberries, raspberries, mango

Five minutes spent preparing these – or, rather, putting together a few ingredients – means that there's a bowl of delicious breakfast ready to greet you in the morning, which could make all the difference to your day. Actually, this is the base recipe from which our modern muesli evolved, so it's almost like going full circle.

You can vary the liquid you use (your favourite plant milk, fruit juice or even just water) and you can add some dried fruit (raisins, prunes, apricots, cranberries, blueberries, sultanas or any others you fancy) to soak in the liquid and become plump overnight.

The next day, you can just eat it as it is, or add any additional ingredients you feel like. A different, delicious treat every day for the minimum of effort.

I find cup measures are easiest for this recipe, and you can adjust them to your taste.

Put the oats, liquid and any dried fruit you fancy into the bowl that you will eat from in the morning. Leave them in the refrigerator overnight to become deliciously soft and creamy.

The next morning, add any extra ingredients you fancy.

muesli

Makes 6 cups (enough for about 6–8 servings)

You can buy all kinds of granolas and muesli mixes, and many of them are suitable for vegans, but you do need to check the label because non-vegan ingredients, such as honey and milk powder, can creep in. Of course, if you're avoiding gluten as well, you'll need to be extra vigilant. If you have the time, why not make your own muesli or granola mix? It's quick and easy, and you'll know exactly what's in it!

Measure by volume, using a cup. A good ratio to use is four parts rolled grains, such as oats, to one part nuts and seeds, plus one part dried fruit. You can vary the mixture to your heart's content and even add a little dried spice, too. It is best to add any sweeteners, such as maple syrup or sugar, to your serving bowl just before you eat it, along with your choice of liquid – vegan milk or fruit juice.

Simply mix everything together and store in an airtight container for 7–10 days. Serve with plant milk to taste, or some people like apple or orange juice, instead. Chopped fresh fruits, such as bananas, raspberries or strawberries, are also good for topping.

note on nuts and seeds ...

For extra flavour, you can toast the nuts and seeds in a moderate oven: spread them out in a single layer in a baking pan and roast them for a few minutes until they smell toasty and are golden. Don't let them overcook – they will continue to roast even when removed from the oven, so take them out in good time and put them on a cold plate to cool. Make sure they are completely cold before adding to your mix.

4 cups grains (choose from: rolled [old-fashioned] oats, quinoa, barley, spelt, rye, millet or puffed rice)

1 cup nuts and seeds, raw or toasted (see Note) (choose from: flaked [slivered] almonds, chopped brazil nuts, cashews, walnuts, pecans, hazelnuts, macadamias; sunflower seeds, sesame seeds, pumpkin seeds)

1 cup dried fruit (choose from: raisins, sultanas [golden raisins], chopped dates, figs, pear, apple, mango, 'cherries and berries' mix, blueberries or any other fruit you fancy)

1–2 pinches salt

1 pinch sweet spice (such as ground cinnamon), or to taste (optional)

For Crunchy Granola:
40g (1½oz/3 tbsp) coconut oil
120ml (4fl oz/½ cup) maple syrup (or golden syrup)
1 tsp salt (optional)
plus all the Muesli ingredients (above)

To serve:
sweetener of choice (such as maple syrup or sugar), to taste (you may not need this for the Granola, as it is already sweetened)
liquid of choice (such as plant milk or fruit juice), to taste

image p.30-31

crunchy granola

The base mix of nuts, seeds and spices for this granola is the same as for the muesli on the opposite page, so why not make a big batch of that, then have it on hand for when you want to serve either recipe.

Preheat the oven to 150°C/300°F/gas mark 2. Line a large baking sheet with greaseproof paper.

Warm the oil, syrup and salt in a saucepan over a gentle heat until they have melted together, then remove from the heat.

Mix all the dry ingredients in a large bowl. Pour in the melted mixture and stir until well combined. Spread the mixture over the baking sheet and bake for 30–35 minutes until golden, stirring occasionally to make sure it cooks evenly.

Cool on the baking sheet (it will become crisp as it does so), then stir in the dried fruit. Store in an airtight container for 7–10 days.

Makes 6 cups (enough for about 6–8 servings)

40g (1½oz/3 tbsp) coconut oil
120ml (4fl oz/½ cup) maple syrup
(or golden syrup)
1 tsp salt (optional)
plus all the Muesli ingredients
(opposite page)

To serve:
sweetener of choice (such as maple
syrup or sugar), to taste (you may
not need this for the Granola,
as it is already sweetened)
liquid of choice (such as plant milk
or fruit juice), to taste

31

quick creamy porridge

for the stove top method

Put the oats into a saucepan along with the liquid and salt, bring to the boil, then reduce the heat and simmer for 5 minutes, stirring from time to time, until the mixture has thickened and the oats have cooked.

for microwave porridge

Put the oats, liquid and salt into a microwave-safe bowl and microwave on high for 5 minutes, stirring halfway through. Leave to stand for 1–2 minutes before eating.

Serve with a sprinkling of sugar, a swirl of maple syrup, a dollop of thick yogurt or coconut cream.

Porridge never goes out of fashion and it's really quick and easy to make, either in a pan on the stovetop or in a microwave. You need the same ingredients whichever method you use. Microwaving takes the same time as making porridge on the stove, just without the stirring.

Either way, it's a delicious, warming breakfast that couldn't be simpler.

Serves 1

50g (2oz/½ cup) porridge oats
350ml (12fl oz/1⅓ cups) liquid of
    choice (your favourite plant milk
    or water, or a mixture)
1 pinch salt

Serving suggestions:
non-dairy cream
thick non-dairy yogurt
coconut cream (see p.244)
sugar
maple syrup
your favourite jam (jelly)

OMELETTES, FRITTATAS AND SCRAMBLES

There are various ways to make vegan versions of scrambles, frittatas and omelettes. The vegan versions of these popular dishes are quick and easy to make, and look and taste surprisingly similar to the traditional eggy originals.

You can use a soft, silky type of tofu, usually bought in a vacuum pack, drained, mashed, coloured with a little turmeric and perhaps bound together with a little cornflour (cornstarch); you can use a batter made from chickpea (gram) flour, which will bind and set; or, for a simple but surprisingly good 'scramble', you can just mash cooked chickpeas. All of these methods are used in the following recipes – try them and see what you think. If you'd like a really 'eggy' flavour, do try adding a pinch or two of Himalayan black salt (kala namak): it's magical and readily available online. You'll be amazed.

tofu omelette

Put the tofu into a food processor or a mixing bowl and add all the other ingredients. You can go easy on the black salt or omit it if you are not sure you will like it. Alternatively, add it gradually, tasting, once the mixture is blended.

Process or mix well until you have a beautifully smooth, pale golden mixture. If it seems very thick, mix in 1 tablespoon water – you want a texture that you can spread easily with the back of a spoon when it's in the pan.

Heat the butter or olive oil in a large frying pan (skillet) over a low heat for about 3 minutes. Pour in the tofu mixture and use a spatula to help spread it over the pan into an omelette shape. Cook for 10–12 minutes, until set, moving it a little with the spatula as it cooks, to prevent it sticking to the pan. Turn it over and cook the other side for 3–5 minutes.

Serve immediately, or top with a delicious filling and fold over to enclose the filling.

Serves 2

225g (8oz) silken tofu (see p.13), liquid discarded but not fully drained
2 garlic cloves, crushed
2 tbsp nutritional yeast
½ tsp ground turmeric
4 tbsp chickpea (gram) flour
1 tbsp cornflour (cornstarch)
2 tbsp light olive oil
1 tsp Himalayan black salt (kala namak), or to taste (optional) (see p.15)
sea salt and freshly ground black pepper, to taste

For shallow-frying:
1–2 tbsp light olive oil or Vegan Butter (Homemade, p.266, or store-bought)

Fillings (optional):
Cheese: some 'Melting Cheese' slices (p.262), 3–4 spoonfuls of 'Cheese' Sauce (p.261), or a little vegan 'Parmesan' (p.263).
Mushroom: fry 50g (2oz) sliced button mushrooms in 1 tbsp vegan butter or olive oil for 2–3 minutes, or until tender.
Asparagus: lightly steam a small handful of tender asparagus tips for 4–5 minutes in a little water in a pan, or in the microwave, until just tender.
Spinach: add a few spoonfuls of cooked spinach leaves.
Fresh herbs: add 2–3 tbsp chopped fresh herbs of your choice: parsley, chives, tarragon, dill.

potato and onion frittata

Place the potatoes in a saucepan with enough water to cover, bring to the boil and cook for 7–10 minutes until just tender, then drain.

Meanwhile, heat 2 tablespoons of the oil in a large frying pan (skillet) over a low-medium heat, add the onions and fry for about 10 minutes, until just tender but not browned.

Add another 2 tablespoons of oil to the frying pan and place the potato slices in an even layer on top of the onions.

Mix together the chickpea (gram) flour, salt, pepper and water to make a smooth batter, then pour it evenly over the potatoes, moving them aside gently to make sure the batter covers them evenly and goes right through to the bottom of the pan.

Continue to cook for 5 minutes or so, until the mixture has set around the edges. Loosen the edges of the frittata, then turn it out on to a large plate, baking sheet or board.

Heat another 2 tablespoons of oil in the frying pan, then slide the frittata back into the pan, and cook for a further 10–15 minutes until the bottom is golden and crisp. This second side tends to look more even and golden than the first side, so you could just lift it out of the pan or you could turn the frittata over again, onto a warmed plate and serve with some mango chutney on the side.

So simple, so delicious – melting, tender potato slices and tasty fried onion encased in a crisp chickpea-flour batter – the perfect dish for brunch or anytime snacking. It does take a little time to cook to perfection, but it's easy to do and well worth it. We love it with mango chutney. You need a large, fairly light frying pan (skillet) that you can turn upside down to flip the frittata over. I love it with some sweet mango chutney and, if there are leftovers, it's also great cold.

Serves 2–4

450g (1lb) potatoes, sliced about 5mm (¼in) thick
90ml (3fl oz/6 tbsp) olive oil
125g (4½oz) red onions, thinly sliced
100g (3½oz/generous ¾ cup) chickpea (gram) flour
1 tsp salt
½ tsp black pepper
300ml (10½fl oz/1¼ cups) water
mango chutney, to serve

tofu scramble

Heat the oil or butter in a medium saucepan over a low-medium heat, add the tofu and sprinkle with the ground turmeric and a light seasoning of salt and pepper. Lightly mash with a fork and gently stir until it resembles scrambled eggs: this only takes a minute or two – don't let it get too dry.

Spoon immediately onto hot buttered toast, top with a scattering of chopped parsley and Himalayan black salt (kala namak), if using and serve immediately.

variation: tofu scramble with mushrooms

Fry 125g (4½oz) cleaned, sliced button mushrooms in 1 tbsp vegan butter or olive oil. Cook over a medium heat for a few minutes until tender, then add the tofu, turmeric and seasoning to the pan and proceed as above.

This is lovely! Being vegan myself, I might be prejudiced, but I think it's a lot nicer than the real scrambled eggs I remember eating as a child.

Serves 2

1 tbsp light olive oil or Vegan Butter (Homemade, p.266, or store-bought)
225g (8oz) silken or medium-firm tofu, drained and patted dry with paper towels
¼ tsp ground turmeric
sea salt and freshly ground black pepper, to taste

To serve

2 slices toast, spread with vegan butter
a little chopped flat-leaf parsley, to garnish
1–2 pinches Himalayan black salt (kala namak), to taste (optional) (see p.15)

image p.44–45

chickpea scramble

Mash the chickpeas in a bowl with a fork, or pulse them in a food processor until they are chunky, then add the spices and mash or pulse again.

Heat the olive oil in a saucepan, add the mashed chickpeas, and the Himalayan black salt (kala namak) if you want an 'eggy' flavour, and stir over the heat for a few minutes before serving.

This is a lovely vegan scramble. It doesn't try to mimic an egg scramble but is delicious in its own right. Serve as it is, or on crisp toast spread with vegan butter (Homemade, p.266, or store-bought).

Serves 2

1 × 400g (14oz) can chickpeas
    (garbanzo beans), drained
½ tsp garlic powder
½ tsp ground cumin
¼ tsp chilli powder
¼ tsp smoked paprika
¼–½ tsp ground turmeric
1 tbsp olive oil
1–2 pinches Himalayan black salt
    (kala namak), to taste (optional)

vegan cooked breakfast

Nothing heralds the arrival of the weekend more than a long, lazy breakfast with family and friends. From shakshuka to pancakes, there are so many great options for a 'cooked' breakfast, but sometimes only the classic full English will do. This is the menu for those days. I haven't included recipes for grilled (broiled) tomatoes and olive oil, but if you want guidance just brush the tomatoes with a little oil and place under a preheated grill (broiler) until juicy and bubbling. Cook the mushrooms in a pan with a little olive oil until beautifully soft and sweet.

sausages (p.116)

tofu scramble (p.38)

vegan 'bacon' (p.41)

vegan steaks (p.42)

fried potatoes (p.43)

grilled (broiled) tomatoes and mushrooms

toast, spread with vegan butter (p.266), to serve

vegan 'bacon'

If you want to make your own vegan bacon quickly at home, from simple, pure ingredients, try this easy recipe based on the marinated tofu that you can buy online or in health stores. This is unbelievably simple to do and hits the spot with bacon-lovers every time. If wished, you could also sprinkle with a few drops of liquid smoke before serving.

Using a very sharp knife, cut the tofu into very thin slices, about 5mm (¼in) thick.

Heat the oil in a frying pan (skillet) over a low-medium heat. Put the tofu slices into the pan in a single layer (you may need to fry them in more than one batch) and fry on both sides until golden, about 4 minutes. They burn quite easily, so take care not to over-cook them. Drain on paper towels, then sprinkle with smoked paprika and soy sauce, to taste.

Serves 4

1 × 215g (7½oz) packet marinated tofu, patted dry with paper towels
2 tbsp olive oil, for frying
smoked paprika and Shoyu-style soy sauce, for sprinkling

vegan steaks

You can buy vegan 'steaks', but it's really easy to make your own. These are based on a wheat gluten mixture and, if you don't want to go to the effort of making your own, I recommend you buy it ready-made. I like the canned braised wheat gluten sold by granoVita under the name Mock Duck (when I had it as a child, it used to be called 'meatless steak', which describes it much better – I don't know why they changed the name). It's available in health stores or online.

These 'steaks' are quick to make and delicious to eat – try serving them with chips and a vegan tartare sauce, for a real treat.

Serves 4

1–2 × 400g (14oz) can/s mock duck (braised wheat gluten), drained and patted completely dry with paper towels
2 tbsp olive oil, for frying

For the marinade:
2 tbsp soy sauce (I like Shoyu-style)
1 tbsp tomato purée (paste)
1 tbsp brown sugar
½ tsp smoked paprika
a few drops of liquid smoke

Mix together all the ingredients for the marinade in a bowl.

Dip the dry pieces of mock duck into the marinade, making sure they are all thoroughly coated.

Heat the olive oil in a frying pan (skillet) over a medium heat. Add the mock duck and shallow fry for about 5 minutes, until thoroughly cooked on both sides. The pieces need to be browned a little, but catch easily because of the sugar, so watch that they don't burn. Serve immediately.

fried potatoes

Golden brown, crisp on the outside and tender within, who doesn't love fried potatoes? And they're so easy to make.

Serves 4

4 medium potatoes, peeled and sliced or cubed, as desired
olive oil, for frying
salt and freshly ground black pepper, to taste

Put the potatoes in a suacepan, cover with water and bring to the boil. Parboil for about 5 minutes until you can pierce the potatoes easily with the point of a knife: this will depend on the size of the pieces; they need to be tender but still firm enough not to break up. Drain well.

Heat a little olive oil in a frying pan (skillet) over a medium heat, then add the potatoes and fry for 10–15 minutes, turning regularly until crisp and golden brown all over. Drain on paper towels and season to taste before serving.

variation

If you already have the oven on, an easy and delicious variation is to slice unpeeled potatoes into slim chip-like wedges, place them on a lightly oiled baking sheet and cook them at 180–200°C/350–400°F/gas mark 4–6 for 20–30 minutes, or until lightly golden brown and tender when pierced with the point of a sharp knife.

45

shakshuka

This 'modern brunch classic' is quick and easy to make and is as good for lunch or supper as for breakfast or brunch. It can have a fiery kick to it; this is a moderate version, but you can increase (or decrease) the heat and spiciness according to your taste. This recipe also multiplies well to feed more people; it's a great way to please a crowd. In my vegan adaptation, I've used a tofu scramble to replace the eggs that usually top this, and the sprinkling of Himalayan black salt (kala namak) gives a beautiful eggy flavour, which deliciously complements the sweetness and fiery kick of the tomato base. All you need is some warm crusty bread for dipping and mopping up the delicious juices.

Heat 1 tablespoon of the olive oil in a shallow ovenproof casserole over a medium heat, add the onion and fry for 5 minutes. Add the red (bell) pepper, cover with a lid, and cook for a further 5 minutes. Remove the lid, add the garlic, paprika or cayenne pepper and tomatoes and cook, uncovered, for about 10–15 minutes until all the vegetables are tender.

Meanwhile, heat the remaining olive oil in a frying pan (skillet) over a low-medium heat, add the tofu pieces and sprinkle with the turmeric. Turn the tofu in the hot oil for a few minutes until heated through and golden brown in places.

Check the seasoning of the tomato mixture, adding salt, pepper, sugar and a dash of lemon juice to taste. Add the Himalayan black salt (kala namak), if wished. Scatter the fried tofu pieces on top, sprinkle with chopped coriander and serve with warm crusty bread.

Serves 2

3 tbsp olive oil

1 onion, chopped

1 red (bell) pepper, deseeded and chopped

3 garlic cloves, crushed

1 tsp mild paprika or cayenne pepper

1 × 400g (14oz) can chopped tomatoes

200g (7oz) soft- or medium-texture plain tofu, drained and torn into rough pieces

½ tsp ground turmeric

sea salt and freshly ground black pepper, to taste

2–3 tsp sugar, to taste

1 tbsp lemon juice, or to taste

1–2 pinches Himalayan black salt (kala namak), to taste

chopped fresh coriander (cilantro), to garnish

warm crusty bread, to serve

pancakes

In a large bowl, mix together the flour, baking powder and salt. Pour in the plant milk and olive oil and mix to make a smooth batter.

Heat 1–2 tbsp olive oil in a frying pan (skillet) over a low-medium heat. Pour off any excess oil onto a saucer. Quickly stir the vinegar into the batter mixture, then pour a little batter into the middle of the pan, tilting the pan to coat it with the batter. Let it cook for about 30 seconds or until the batter has set and you can lift the edge to see if it has brown spots on it. Flip the pancake over (use a wide spatula if necessary), cook the other side for a few seconds, then remove the pancake to a serving plate.

Fry the remaining batter in the same way, adding more oil as needed.

variations: thicker, wrap-style pancakes

Make the batter as above, but use 130–150 ml (4½–5fl oz/ generous ½–⅔ cup) milk. You want a batter that will pour, but needs to be eased over the pan a little with a spatula. Once the underside has cooked, be ready to flip the pancake over and cook the other side. Makes 3–4.

american-style pancakes

Make the batter as above, but use 100ml (3½fl oz/scant ½ cup) milk. Drop small amounts of the batter into the frying pan to make little round puffy pancakes and fry them for a little longer on each side to allow the batter to cook through. They are delicious served with maple syrup or tender, sweet fruits, such as ripe mango. Makes about 6.

You can make lovely pancakes without using any eggs or dairy milk. The basic recipe makes thin, English-style pancakes. If you make the batter with less milk, you can spread it over the pan and cook it for a bit longer to make thicker, 'wrap-style' pancakes; or use an even thicker batter to make lovely American-style, small puffy pancakes.

Makes 6 large pancakes

100g (3½oz/¾ cup) plain (all-purpose) flour
1 tsp baking powder
¼ tsp salt
200ml (7fl oz/scant 1 cup) plant-based milk
2 tbsp mild olive oil, plus extra for frying
1 tsp cider vinegar or wine vinegar

ON TOAST

Fast to make, crunchy, tasty and satisfying, who doesn't love a simple hot snack on a piece of crisp toast? There are some delicious vegan options; here are some of my favourites:

'cheese' on toast

Preheat the grill (broiler) to hot.

Toast the bread under the hot grill, then place the slices of 'Melting Cheese' on top. Alternatively, spoon the 'Cheese Sauce' on top, if that's what you're using. Place back under the grill for a few minutes until the cheese is lightly browned and melting.

Scatter with a little chopped parsley and serve.

This makes a beautiful, tasty snack that hits all the spots and is very quick and simple to make. The 'cheese' takes about 30 minutes to make, but keeps well in the refrigerator, in the same way that store-bought soft cheese keeps, for about a week. I like to use this 'cheese' as it contains only pure, simple ingredients, but you could also use a store-bought 'melting' vegan cheese, if you prefer.

Serves 1

1–2 slices bread
½ x recipe quantity 'Melting Cheese' (see p.262), sliced, or ¼ x recipe quantity 'Cheese Sauce' (p.261)
chopped fresh flat-leaf parsley, to serve

chilli avocado on sourdough toast

This is lovely – creamy avocado with a kick of hot chilli and some fresh coriander (cilantro) leaves on crisp toast.

Serves 1–2

1 medium or ½ large avocado, pitted and flesh removed 1 tbsp fresh lemon juice
sea salt and freshly ground black pepper
2 large slices white sourdough bread
hot red chilli sauce or Tabasco sauce, to taste
chopped fresh coriander (cilantro), to serve

Coarsely mash the avocado flesh in a bowl with the lemon juice and add salt and pepper to taste.

Toast the bread.

Divide the mashed avocado between the toast, sprinkle with a few drops of hot red chilli sauce (to taste – go carefully!) and scatter with a little chopped fresh coriander (cilantro).

wild mushrooms on sourdough toast

This is one of my favourite speedy light meals or anytime snack. I like it best when made with organic white sourdough bread and whatever 'wild' mushrooms I can buy, but it's also delicious made with regular mushrooms, especially when they're fried in vegan butter (Homemade, p.266, or store-bought). So simple, so good.

Heat the olive oil or vegan butter in a frying pan (skillet) over a medium heat. Add the mushrooms and fry for about 5 minutes, or until tender and lightly browned.

Meanwhile toast the bread – it's best not to let it get too crisp, so that the mushrooms will sit on it better.

Season the mushrooms with a little salt and pepper, then spoon them on top of the toast and scatter with a little chopped parsley.

Serves 1–2

1–2 tbsp olive oil or Vegan Butter
    (Homemade, p.266,
    or store-bought)
300g (10½oz) mixed wild mushrooms
    or firm baby mushrooms, cleaned,
    dried and sliced
2 large slices white sourdough bread
sea salt and freshly ground black
    pepper
chopped fresh flat-leaf parsley,
    to serve

STUFFED WRAPS

Stuffed with delicious fillings, wraps are wonderful for breakfast, brunch or lunch – in fact, they're an ideal anytime portable meal. Wraps or pitta breads are widely available to buy or, alternatively, you could make a thicker version of the pancakes (p.48). For the fillings: anything goes, but it's good to include something soft that will help to hold it all together; something crisp, for texture; and something fresh and juicy. If you're catering for a crowd, you can lay out some wraps and bowls of delicious, varied ingredients and let people roll their own.

Filling and Topping Ideas:

- Fast and Easy Roasted Summer Vegetables (p.82)
- Chickpea Scramble (p.39)
- Vegan Bacon (p.41)
- Homemade Mayonnaise (p.258)
- hot chilli sauce of choice
- 1 avocado, sliced
- baby salad leaves
- Hummus (p.64), falafel and salad
- Hummus (p.64), grated carrot and coriander (cilantro)
- Cannellini Bean Dip with Red Pepper Sauce (p.66)

burritos

Heat the olive oil in a saucepan over a medium heat, add the onion, (bell) pepper and garlic and fry for about 10 minutes, until tender, then add the red kidney beans, chopped tomatoes and chilli powder.

Soften and warm the tortilla wraps by popping them under a warm grill (broiler) or microwaving them for 1–2 minutes.

Lay each tortilla on a flat surface and arrange some filling at the base of the tortilla. Add any optional extras you wish, leaving room around the edges for the filling to expand as you fold and roll it. Fold the two sides in over the filling, then fold the bottom up to enclose the filling and roll gently, to form a neat cylinder – and it's done.

Burittos – wraps filled with delicious ingredients, baked and served warm or hot – are a great quick breakfast, brunch or anytime snack. There are no rules, really; all you need is a pack of wraps, a few tasty ingredients and 10–15 minutes to spare. Sliced fried onion and red (bell) pepper with some slightly mashed red kidney beans and chopped fresh or canned tomato makes a good basis for the filling, along with some salad leaves.

Serves 4

2 tbsp olive oil
1 onion, chopped
1 red (bell) pepper, deseeded and chopped
1 garlic clove, crushed
1 × 400g (14oz) can red kidney beans, drained
1 × 400g (14oz) can chopped tomatoes
1 tsp chilli powder, or to taste
4 wholemeal flour tortillas

To serve (optional):
1 avocado, sliced
vegan soured cream
grated vegan cheese
rocket (arugula) or other salad leaves, to garnish

light bites and lunches

SANDWICHES AND TOPPED CROSTINI

Sandwiches: where would we be without them?! They really are the most convenient way to make, and eat, a quick snack, and vegan varieties can be very delicious as well as healthy. One of the secrets to a good sandwich is to use nicely soft and springy bread (white and/or brown) then, unless the filling does not require it, I like to spread the bread with my Vegan Butter (see p.266) and top with a generous amount of delicious filling. As a change from sandwiches, crostini are lovely, too: perhaps not as practical to transport and eat, but so pretty and tempting, and quick to assemble once you've made the bases, which can be done in advance, as described on p.62.

Filling and Topping Ideas:

- Vegan Cream Cheese (p.263) and thinly sliced cucumber
- Vegan Cream Cheese (p.263) and Chutney
- Hummus (p.64), black olive and coriander (cilantro)
- Hummus (p.64) and roasted red (bell) pepper
- Hummus (p.64), cooked sliced beetroot and dill
- Moroccan Hummus: Hummus (p.64) sprinkled with Za'atar (p.268) or Ras al Hanout (p.268).
- peanut butter and sliced banana or raisins
- peanut butter and jam (jelly)
- peanut butter and salad, such as grated carrot, spring onion (scallion), chopped celery or salad leaves
- Vegan BLT: Seitan 'Bacon' (p.41), thinly-sliced smoked tofu, or tofu fried and drizzled with shoyu, with lettuce and sliced tomato
- Vegan 'Tuna' (see recipe, right)
- 'Egg Mayonnaise' (see recipe, right)
- sliced avocado, tender baby salad leaves and a little sliced tomato
- Asparagus Rolls: thinly cut soft brown bread spread with Vegan Butter (p.266) rolled around a spear of cooked asparagus
- Canellini, Sundried Tomato and Basil: canned cannellini beans, drained and roughly mashed with sundried tomato purée and a few shredded basil leaves, to taste
- White Bean Hummus (p.66) with sliced artichoke hearts
- Chickpea Scramble (p.39)
- Quick Guacamole (p.68) or use this abbreviated recipe: using a fork, coarsely mash 1 ripe avocado, adding salt and a dash of Tabasco or other hot pepper sauce to taste; top with chopped fresh coriander (cilantro) and/or finely chopped red (bell) pepper.
- Spicy Salsa Crostini Topping (see p.62)
- Cream Cheese, Spinach, Caramelized Onion and Pomegranate Crostini Topping (see p.63)

vegan 'tuna'

Brought up as a vegetarian, I have never eaten tuna, but I have it on the good authority of those who have that this recipe 'hits the tuna spot' for them. I must say, I really love it, both as a sandwich filling and as part of a salad plate.

Process the jackfruit, nori and mayonnaise in a food processor until you have a flaky, tuna-like mixture. Season with a dash of vinegar and salt to taste.

Makes enough for 4 generous sandwiches

1 × 400g (14oz) can jackfruit in water, drained
2 sheets nori seaweed, roughly torn
2 tbsp vegan mayonnaise, Homemade (see p.258) or store-bought
2 tsp wine or cider vinegar
salt, to taste

'egg mayonnaise'

Mash the tofu with the vegan mayonnaise, mustard, turmeric and nutritional yeast, if using. Season with salt and pepper. If you want a more 'eggy' flavour, add a pinch or two of kala namak.

Makes enough for 4 sandwiches

1 × 225–250g block firm tofu
5–6 tbsp vegan mayonnaise, Homemade (see p.258) or store-bought
½–1 tsp vegan mustard
½–1 tsp ground turmeric
2 tsp nutritional yeast flakes (optional)
1–2 pinches Himalayan black salt (kala namak) (see p.15) (optional)
salt and freshly ground black pepper, to taste

spicy salsa with avocado crostini topping

Makes enough for about 12 crostini

1 garlic clove, crushed

1 medium red onion, very finely chopped

3 tomatoes, very finely chopped

a small handful of fresh coriander (cilantro), finely chopped

½ tsp chilli powder

½ tsp ground cumin

juice of 1 lime

flesh of 1 medium avocado, roughly mashed

12 crostini bases, to serve

First make the salsa: mix together the garlic, onion and tomatoes (a food processor is good for this), then stir in the coriander (cilantro), chilli powder, ground cumin and lime juice.

Thickly spread the mashed avocado over the crostini bases and top each with a spoonful of spicy salsa.

note on crostini ...

Home-made crostini couldn't be simpler to make. Simply slice baguette into 5mm/¼in rounds, brush both sides with a little olive oil and season with salt and pepper. Spread the crostini on a baking sheet and bake at 200°C/400°F/gas mark 6 for 15–20 minutes, turning them over halfway through, until both sides are crisp and just starting to turn golden. Spread the baked crostini with toppings of your choice and serve.

cream 'cheese' and caramelized onion crostini topping

Makes enough for 12 crostini

2 red onions, finely sliced
1 tbsp olive oil
1 × 125g (4½oz) packet baby spinach
    leaves
125–150g (4½–5½oz) Vegan Cream
    Cheese (p.263), for spreading
ground cumin, for sprinkling
pomegranate seeds, for sprinkling
salt and freshly ground black pepper,
    to taste

Heat the oil in a frying pan (skillet) over a low-medium heat, add the onion and fry for 10 minutes until caramelized.

Meanwhile, briefly cook the spinach leaves until wilted.

Spread each crostini base with a little vegan 'cream cheese', top with a little of the spinach and onions, then season to taste with some salt and pepper and a pinch of ground cumin. Finally, add a scattering of jewel-bright pomegranate seeds.

QUICK DIPS

speedy hummus

I love making and eating dips; they are so easy to whizz up and so versatile! Great served on individual plates as starters, decorated attractively with fresh salad, chopped herbs, a sprinkling of spices, a swirl of olive oil or some olives (as appropriate). They can also be served as light meals in themselves or sandwich fillings or served with drinks. Some can even be served as a 'sauce' or a side with a hot main course.

Although hummus is widely available, it's very easy to make your own. You can also save the liquid from the chickpeas (garbanzo beans) – known as 'aquafaba' (see p.13) – for its use in other recipes, such as Meringues (see p.244).

Serves 2–4

1 × 400g (14oz) can chickpeas (garbanzo beans), drained and liquid reserved
1 tbsp olive oil
1 tbsp tahini
1 garlic clove, crushed
1–2 tbsp fresh lemon juice
sea salt, to taste

Put the chickpeas and 2–3 tablespoons of their reserved liquid into a food processor or the goblet of a hand-held (immersion) blender, along with the olive oil, tahini, garlic and lemon juice. Process until smooth, adding more liquid as necessary to obtain the creamy texture you prefer. Taste and add a little salt or lemon juice, as necessary.

variations
I like to spread the hummus out on a plate to a depth of about 1cm (½in), then top it with one of the following:

- a swirl of olive oil and a sprinkling of paprika
- fresh pomegranate seeds and coriander (cilantro) leaves
- a sprinkling of either of the za'atar or ras al hanout (p.268)

cannellini bean dip with red pepper sauce and sesame broccoli

Here's another variation of a bean-based dip, which makes a very pretty and delicious first course. You can make the red pepper sauce in advance.

Serves 2

For the dip:
1 × 400g (14oz) can cannellini beans, drained and liquid reserved
1 garlic clove
juice of ½–1 lemon
sea salt and freshly ground black pepper, to taste

For the red pepper sauce:
1 red (bell) pepper, deseeded and finely chopped
1 tbsp olive oil
1 pinch sugar
sea salt, to taste

For the sesame broccoli:
225g (8oz) sprouting broccoli, trimmed
1–2 tbsp toasted sesame seeds or gomasio seasoning (see p.268)

To make the dip, put the beans and 2–3 tablespoons of their reserved liquid into a food processor or the goblet of a hand-held (immersion) blender, along with the garlic. Process until smooth, adding more liquid as necessary to get a smooth, creamy texture. Mix in lemon juice and seasoning, to taste.

To make the red pepper sauce, put the red (bell) pepper into a pan with about 1cm (½in) depth of water, bring to the boil, then reduce the heat to low and simmer for about 15 minutes, or until the pepper is very tender. Drain and transfer to a food processor, along with the olive oil, sugar and a little salt, to taste, and purée until smooth.

Cook the broccoli in a saucepan with a little boiling water for a few minutes, until only just tender. Drain and set aside.

Serve the dip with the red pepper sauce and broccoli with a good sprinkling of toasted sesame seeds or gomasio seasoning.

guacamole

One of my favourite quick dips, this adds a touch of luxury to any salad meal and is perfect served as a dip with crisps or tortilla chips (see below), or celery sticks, spring onions (scallions) and small pieces of cauliflower.

Cut the avocado in half, twist the two halves apart, remove the stone and peel off and discard the skin.

Mash the avocado in a bowl with a fork, for a chunky texture (which I like), or with a hand-held (immersion) blender, if you want it smoother, adding the lemon juice, Tabasco and seasoning to taste.

Serve on a plate, generously scattered with chopped fresh coriander (cilantro).

Serves 2–4

1 large, ripe avocado
1–2 tbsp fresh lemon juice
dash of Tabasco sauce
sea salt and freshly ground black
    pepper
2–3 sprigs fresh coriander (cilantro),
    to serve

note
Choose your avocado carefully, as the quality of the dip depends upon it; it should yield a little when you press it gently, neither too soft nor too hard. If you don't like coriander (cilantro), this is also lovely served with some fresh basil or chopped chives.

tortilla chips

Preheat the oven to 180°C/350°F/gas mark 4 and grease a couple of baking sheets with olive oil.

Brush olive oil over the surface of one of the tortillas. Place another tortilla on top and brush it too with olive oil. Continue in this way until you have piled them all up. Cut the pile of tortillas into eighths, so you end up with numerous small triangles

Spread the triangles over the baking sheets and bake for 8 minutes or until golden – don't let them get too brown.

Cool on the sheets before serving. They are best when freshly made, but once cool they can be stored in an airtight container for a few days. If storing, pop them into a hot oven again for a few minutes before serving.

Serves 4–6

olive oil, for brushing
1 packet corn tortilla wraps (containing
    at least 6–8 wraps)

quick creamy butterbean dip

This lovely smooth and creamy dip is very easy to make and is a nice change from hummus. You can eat it as it is, but try it swirled with a little chilli sauce and topped with chopped parsley. You could use a store-bought hot red pepper sauce, such as sriracha.

Serves 2–4

1 × 400g (14oz) can butter (lima) beans, drained and liquid reserved
1 garlic clove, crushed
1–2 tbsp fresh lemon juice, to taste
hot red pepper sauce, to taste
sea salt, to taste
chopped flat-leaf parsley, to garnish

Put the butter beans and 2–3 tablespoons of their reserved liquid into a food processor or the goblet of a hand-held (immersion) blender, along with the garlic. Process until smooth, adding more liquid as necessary to get a smooth, creamy texture. Alternatively, for a coarser texture, you can mash the beans and garlic roughly with a fork, adding a little of the reserved liquid as you go.

Mix in a little lemon juice and hot red pepper sauce – just a few drops at a time – and a little salt, as necessary, tasting as you go.

Scatter with a little chopped parsley to serve.

Whether you are just looking for a light, snacky lunch, or just something to get you through the long afternoon, the recipes on the following pages are the perfect pick-up-able pick-me-ups for any time hunger strikes.

crispy chickpeas

Since the liquid in a can of chickpeas (garbanzo beans) is so useful as a stand-in for whisked egg whites (see p.244), ideas for using up chickpeas are useful – and these are delicious.

Prehat the oven to 200°C/400°F/gas mark 6. Pour the olive oil into a roasting tin (pan) and place in the oven to heat up.

Blot the drained chickpeas (garbanzo beans) with paper towels to dry them, then toss them in the chickpea (gram) flour.

Remove the hot tin from the oven and add the chickpeas, turning them gently to coat in the hot oil. Roast for about 15 minutes or until golden brown, then turn off the heat and leave them in the oven for a further 5 minutes or so to finish crisping up.

Let cool, then sprinkle with a little salt before serving, if you like.

1 tbsp olive oil
1 × 400g (14oz) can chickpeas (garbanzo beans), drained
1–2 tbsp chickpea (gram) flour
sea salt, to taste (optional)

celeriac chips with garlic mayo

Preheat the oven to 200°C/400°F/gas mark 6.

Meanwhile, using a sharp knife, peel the celeriac (I find it best to stand it on a board and cut downwards, taking off fairly thick slices of skin). You should end up with about 500g (1lb 2oz) celeriac.

Cut the celeriac into chunky chips.

Place the chips into a shallow roasting pan, drizzle over the olive oil, ensuring each chip is evenly coated, then spread them out in a single layer and season with salt.

Bake for about 25 minutes, or until the chips are golden brown and crisp at the edges.

Serve immediately, with Aioli for dipping (see p.258).

Celeriac chips (fries) have a lovely naturally salty flavour and make a nice appetizer or snack.

Serves 4

1 celeriac (celery root) (buying weight about 700g/1lb 9oz)
3 tbsp olive oil
sea salt, to taste
Aioli (p.258), to serve

grilled 'halloumi' platter

To make the 'halloumi', drain the tofu, blot dry with paper towels, then cut it into slices about 7mm (¼in) thick. Lay them out in a single layer on a flat plate.

Mix the olive oil with the garlic and dried mint, then spoon it over the tofu slices and rub it in, until both sides are coated. Set aside to marinate for 30–60 minutes (longer if you can).

Heat a ridged griddle pan until sizzling hot (test by dripping a drop of water on to it). Using tongs, lower the pieces of tofu onto the griddle pan, pressing them down slightly to make sure they are sitting firmly on the ridges.

Griddle for 5–10 minutes, until deep-brown char marks appear, then turn them over and griddle the other side. Once you have the char marks on both sides, if the griddle pan is set over a very low heat you can leave the tofu in place for quite a long time as long as it's not browing or getting burnt – this seems to improve the flavour.

Meanwhile, for the tzatziki, just mix together the yogurt and mint, season with a little salt and put into a small shallow serving bowl.

Serve with the sliced tomatoes, olives, a scattering of mint leaves and a sprinkle of sea salt, to taste. Serve the tzatziki and some toasted pitta bread on the side.

If you buy a really firm tofu, you can marinade it in olive oil and garlic, then griddle it until it has some deep-brown markings on it – the taste and texture is very similar to that of halloumi cheese. Add some minty tzatziki, a simple tomato salad, black olives and toasted pitta bread, and you could be sitting at a Greek taverna on a balmy night: listening to the lapping water, seeing the reflection of the harbour lights and watching the stars coming out.

Serves 2 as a main course,
4 as a starter or side

For the 'halloumi':
1 × 280g (10oz) pack firm plain tofu
2 tbsp olive oil
1 garlic clove, crushed
1–2 teaspoons dried mint

For the tzatziki:
4 heaped tbsp plain vegan yogurt
1 tbsp chopped fresh mint
sea salt, to taste

To serve:
2 tomatoes, sliced
1–2 handfuls black Kalamata olives
handful of fresh mint leaves
sea salt, to taste
toasted pitta bread

easy vegan sushi with avocado

I love sushi. It makes a great anytime snack, starter or light meal and looks far more complicated to make than it is. It's nice served with pickled ginger and some hot wasabi paste, which you can buy ready-made from any large supermarket.

Place the rice in a saucepan with the water and bring to the boil, uncovered. Cover, reduce the heat and cook for about 12 minutes, or until the water is absorbed and the rice cooked. Allow to cool for a few minutes, then stir in the rice vinegar and sugar. You can use the rice to make the sushi as soon as it's cool enough to handle.

To make the sushi rolls, place a piece of nori, shiny-side down, on a board and lightly cover it with the rice, leaving a 1-cm (½-in) gap at the end farthest from you. Place a row of red (bell) pepper strips on top of the rice, at the end closest to you, about 2.5cm (1in) from the edge. Lay some asparagus spears next to the red pepper and a line of avocado strips next to that. Fold over the edge of the nori closest to you, quite firmly, then continue to roll the nori up, like a Swiss roll. Continue to make sushi rolls in this way until all the ingredients have been used up, then refrigerate until required.

To serve, trim the two ends of each roll (these tend to be a little untidy), then cut the rolls into 4 or 5 pieces. Place them, filling-side up, on a serving plate and sprinkle with a few toasted sesame seeds, if you like. Serve with the soy sauce for dipping – it's nice to give each person their own tiny bowl of sauce – and some wasabi paste and pickled ginger.

Makes 16–20 pieces

225g (8oz/scant 1¼ cups) sushi rice
   or pudding rice
300ml (10½ fl oz/1¼ cups) water
2 tsp rice vinegar or wine vinegar
2 tsp caster (superfine) sugar
4–5 sheets of nori seaweed
1 red (bell) pepper, deseeded
   and cut into long strips
4–5 asparagus spears, cooked
   and drained
flesh of 1 avocado, cut into long strips
salt and freshly ground black pepper,
   to taste

To serve:
toasted sesame seeds, to garnish
   (optional)
soy sauce, for dipping
pickled ginger, to taste
wasabi paste, to taste

77

falafel

Put the millet into a saucepan along with the water and a big pinch of salt and bring to the boil. Reduce the heat, cover and simmer for 15–20 minutes, until the millet is tender and fluffy and all the water has been absorbed.

Transfer the cooked millet to a food processor and add the chickpeas, parsley, garlic, spring onion (scallions) and coriander (cilantro). Process until just combined but still chunky. If you prefer, you can do this by hand – put the chickpeas into a bowl and mash roughly, then add the millet and other ingredients and mix until it holds together. Season well with salt.

Form the mixture into flat rounds.

Heat the olive oil in a frying pan (skillet) over a medium heat, add the falafel and fry for about 3 minutes on each side until golden brown and crisp. Drain on paper towels, then serve warm or cold.

These are lovely served with the Lettuce, Olive and Avocado Salad (p.90) and a good-quality, preferably organic, store-bought hummus (or you can whizz some up in about 5 minutes – see p.64).

Serves 4 (makes about 10)

120g (4½oz/½ cup) raw millet
250ml (9fl oz/1 cup) water
sea salt, to taste
1 × 400g (14oz) can chickpeas (garbanzo beans), drained and patted dry with paper towels
handful of flat-leaf parsley
1 garlic clove, crushed
2 spring onions (scallions), finely sliced
1 tsp ground coriander
2 tbsp olive oil, for frying

*image
p.78-79*

EASY VEG

A beautiful plate of vegetables can brighten up even the dreariest of days. The recipes on the following pages are packed with flavour and require minimal effort, making them the perfect quick lunch for those times when you want something delicious and nutritious but haven't got the time or energy to spend hours in the kitchen.

roasted winter vegetables

These lovely winter vegetables roasted in olive oil and maple syrup are very quick to put together. Serve with cauliflower couscous (or regular couscous), or with a dollop of Hummus (p.64), or with tender-stem broccoli (put it on to cook when you add the beets to the roast vegetables).

Preheat the oven to 180°C/350°F/gas mark 4.

Put the carrots, parsnips and onions into a roasting pan, drizzle over the olive oil and maple syrup and season with salt and pepper. Roast for 30 minutes. Add the cooked beetroot (beet) to the pan, mix gently and roast for a further 10 minutes.

Serves 2

250g (9oz) carrots, cut into fingers
250g (9oz) parsnips, cut into fingers
2 red onions, each cut into 8 wedges
3–4 tbsp olive oil
3 tbsp maple syrup
1–2 pre-cooked beetroot (beets), cut into fingers
salt and freshly ground black pepper, to taste

fast and easy roasted summer vegetables

Preheat the oven to 190°C/375°F/gas mark 5.

Place the pepper, courgette, aubergine and onion pieces into a roasting pan, drizzle with the olive oil, and bake in the oven for 20–30 minutes, or until lightly browned and tender to the point of a knife.

Remove the pan from the oven, add the cherry tomatoes and garlic to the pan, and return to the oven to bake for a further 10–15 minutes.

Scatter with fresh basil leaves and serve.

About the easiest and most labour-saving way that I know of producing a beautiful platter of delicious vegetables! And they're so versatile; beautiful just on their own as a light meal, but also great as an easy and colourful accompaniment to a more substantial main dish such as a nut roast or burgers. If there's any left over, which – admittedly – is unlikely in my house, they're also tasty to eat cold.

Serves 2 as a light meal or 4 as an accompaniment

1 red (bell) pepper, deseeded and
    sliced into bite-size pieces
1 yellow pepper, deseeded and sliced
    into bite-size pieces
1 medium courgette (zucchini),
    trimmed and cut into bite-size
    pieces
1 medium aubergine (eggplant),
    trimmed and cut into bite-size
    pieces
1 red onion, sliced
1–2 tbsp olive oil
200g (7oz) cherry tomatoes
4 garlic cloves, sliced
fresh basil leaves, to garnish

jacket potatoes

Preheat the oven to 230°C/450°F/gas mark 8: this is important.

Prick each potato 2 or 3 times with a fork, then roll in some fine sea salt so that they pick up a fine coating.

Put the potatoes into the hot oven, directly on the rack if you can, and bake for at least 1 hour, until they feel just tender when you give them a squeeze, and have a crisp skin. If they are not ready, leave them for a few minutes longer, then test again: don't leave them so long that they dry out.

Serve the potatoes straight out onto plates without breaking the skin – this is best done by the person who is going to eat the potato, straight out of the oven and moments before they take the first delicious mouthful.

Everyone loves a jacket potato – it's cheap, very quick to prepare and simple to cook. There are three things to remember to get it perfect every time: use a floury variety of potato (Estima, Maris Piper, King Edward or Desiree); bake it in a very hot oven; and eat it at once, while it's still gloriously crisp and crunchy. So, get your fillings or toppings prepared while the potato cooks, then be ready to drop everything and enjoy it as soon as it's done.

Serves 1

1 potato per person, washed and dried
fine sea salt, for rolling

Serving suggestions:
Homemade Vegan Butter (p.266) (my favourite, or a store-bought one if you prefer)
vegan 'hard cheese', grated
pesto (you can buy good vegan pesto; or see p.96 for a recipe for homemade pesto)
Hummus (p.64)
Vegan Mayonnaise (p.258) (easy to do and definitely worth the effort
salad leaves (I prefer just to enjoy the steaming hot, crunchy-skinned potato, but some mixed leaves – purple, green, different shapes and sizes – go well with it if you like them, and look pretty on the plate)

baked sweet potatoes with a crispy coating

This is a lovely way to cook sweet potatoes: coated with an easy chickpea-flour batter and crunchy breadcrumbs, then baked crisp and golden in the oven. Serve with refreshing rocket (arugula) and creamy hummus.

Serves 1

For each serving:
1 medium slender sweet potato

For the coating:
1–2 tbsp chickpea (gram) flour
1 small pinch salt
2–4 tbsp cold water
2–4 tbsp dry breadcrumbs
olive oil, for baking

To serve:
handful of rocket (arugula) leaves
1–2 tbsp hummus, Homemade (p.64)
    or store-bought

Preheat the oven to 200°C/400°F/gas mark 6. Pour a little olive oil into a shallow roasting tin. If the sweet potato has a blemish-free skin, you can simply wash it and pat dry; otherwise – and I think this is best in any case – peel it thinly using a potato peeler. Cut into 2cm (¾in) rounds.

Mix the chickpea (gram) flour in a bowl with a light seasoning of salt and enough cold water to make a thick batter. Set the breadcrumbs on a piece of foil or baking paper nearby. Dip the pieces of sweet potato first into the batter, coating them all over as much as possible, then into the breadcrumbs.

Carefully put the pieces of coated sweet potato into the roasting tin, turning them in the oil to coat them all over. Bake for about 20 minutes until crisp, crunchy and golden brown.

Serve immediately, with rocket (arugula) and hummus.

crisp oven-baked aubergine fritters

Preheat the oven to 180°C/350°F/gas mark 4. Put a roasting pan that will hold all the aubergine (eggplant) slices in a single layer into the oven to heat up.

Prepare three dipping bowls: put the plant milk into one bowl; the cornflour (cornstarch) into the next; and a mixture of the panko breadcrumbs, sesame seeds, garlic and onion powders into the third.

Dip each slice of aubergine first in the milk, then into the cornflour, and finally into the panko mix, so that each is generously coated.

Carefully pour the olive oil into the hot roasting pan, then use tongs to place the coated aubergine slices into the oil, turning them so that they get lightly coated with oil on both sides. Bake for about 20 minutes, turning the slices halfway through, until they are crisp and golden brown. Lightly sprinkle with a little sea salt before serving, if you like.

This is a quick and easy recipe for these crisp oven-baked aubergine (eggplant) slices, which taste as though they have been battered and deep-fried. They make a lovely snack, or you can add a handful of rocket (arugula) leaves and perhaps a few oven-baked chips (fries) to make more of a meal of it. They're delicious served with the Quick Creamy Caper Sauce (p.156), which you can mix up while they're in the oven.

Serves 2

1 aubergine (eggplant), cut into 5-mm (¼-in) thick slices
4–5 tbsp olive oil
sea salt, to serve (optional)

For the coating:
4 tbsp cornflour (cornstarch) 4 tbsp plant milk
40g (1½oz/1 cup) panko breadcrumbs
2 tbsp sesame seeds
½ tsp garlic powder
½ tsp onion powder

sweet roasted cauliflower with sumac

The combination of cauliflower, olive oil, maple syrup and the red spice sumac, with its addictive, lemony flavour, makes this dish as pretty to look at as it tastes good to eat. I find that the strength of sumac varies with the brand – it's worth getting a really good one. I love sumac and tend to put a lot on!

Preheat the oven to 180°C/350°F/gas mark 4.

Spread the cauliflower slices in a single layer over a baking sheet, drizzle with the olive oil and maple syrup, ensuring the slices are well coated, then sprinkle with about ½ tsp sumac and a little salt to taste.

Roast for about 25 minutes, or until the cauliflower is just tender and browning at the edges.

Arrange on your serving plates, tuck some rocket (arugula) all round the edges and sprinkle the cauliflower with extra sumac, to taste.

Serves 2 as a light meal or
4 as a side dish

500g (1lb 2 oz) cauliflower florets
    (roughly 2 large cauliflowers), sliced
    thinly so they lie flat
2 tbsp olive oil
4 tbsp maple syrup
sumac, to taste
sea salt, to taste
handful of fresh rocket (arugula),
    to serve

leeks in vinaigrette

Tender, slim baby leeks, cooked until tender and dressed with this piquant marinade, make an unusual and appetising starter.

Bring a 1cm (½in) depth of water to the boil in a saucepan, add the baby leeks and cook for about 8 minutes, until they are just tender to the point of a knife. Drain and plunge into cold water to stop the cooking process, then drain again.

Divide the leeks between two serving plates.

Mix together the olive oil, red wine vinegar and a good pinch of salt, then drizzle over the leeks. Sprinkle with a little chopped parsley, and serve.

Serves 2

125g (4½oz) slim baby leeks, washed and trimmed if necessary
4 tbsp olive oil
2 tbsp red wine vinegar
a good pinch of sea salt
a little chopped flat-leaf parsley, to garnish

lettuce, olive and avocado salad

This is an easy, refreshing starter or anytime snack. The combination of the colourful leaves, green and black olives, and buttery avocado is pretty and appetising as well as delicious.

Make the dressing: combine the ingredients in a glass jar with a lid and shake, or whisk together in a cup or small bowl.

Divide the salad leaves between serving plates, then top with the avocado slices and the green and black olives. Drizzle a little dressing over each plate and serve.

Serves 4

140g (5oz) mixed green and purple salad leaves
1 medium, ripe avocado, pitted, peeled and sliced
handful each green and black olives, pitted

For the dressing:
2 tsp Dijon mustard
4 tbsp olive oil
2 tbsp red wine vinegar
2 tbsp water
1 tsp salt

asparagus with shoyu and sesame seeds

Such a simple and refreshing way to serve asparagus! It's particularly lovely as a starter to an Eastern-style meal, such as Persian Pilaf (p.169) or Aubergine Pilaf Cake (p.196).

Serves 2

125g (4½oz) slim asparagus or asparagus tips, washed and trimmed if necessary
1–2 tbsp shoyu soy sauce
1–2 tsp toasted sesame seeds

Bring a 1cm (½in) depth of water to the boil in a saucepan, add the asparagus and cook for about 3 minutes (if slim), or 5–7 minutes, or even longer (if thick), until they are just tender to the point of a knife. Drain and plunge into cold water to stop the cooking process, then drain again.

Divide the asparagus between two serving plates, drizzle with the shoyu and sprinkle with the sesame seeds.

93

cauliflower couscous

Serves 2 as a main course, 4 as a side

450–500g (1lb–1lb 2oz) cauliflower
  florets
100g (3½oz) carrots, coarsely sliced
1 red (bell) pepper, deseeded and
  coarsely chopped
½ red onion, cut into chunks
handful of flat-leaf parsley
1 tbsp olive oil
1 tbsp cider vinegar
1 tbsp maple syrup
sea salt, to taste
handful of raisins and/or black olives
  (optional)
2–3 tbsp water or vegan stock (broth),
  to cook

I love Cauliflower Steaks, but you only get two good 'steaks' from one cauliflower, leaving you with the dilemma of what to do with the remaining vegetable. You could make one of my absolute favourite dishes, Sweet Roasted Cauliflower with Sumac (p.88), or you could try this equally delicious cauliflower couscous – cauliflower grated or chopped in a food processor so that it resembles couscous grains – mixed with other delicious veg. I find this is very popular, even with people who think that they're not that keen on vegetables, and you can use your own colourful mixture of vegetables, spices, dried fruits, nuts and herbs. Here is one of my favourite combinations.

Put the cauliflower florets into a food processor and pulse briefly until they are beginning to break down. Add the carrot, red pepper, onion and parsley, and pulse until the mixture looks like couscous with flecks of coloured vegetables in it – be careful not to over-process. Add the olive oil, vinegar, maple syrup and some salt to taste, and process again very briefly until mixed in. Stir in the raisins and/or black olives.

Transfer the mixture to a saucepan, add the water or stock and cook, covered, for about 10 minutes over a low-medium heat (a little more water can be added if it gets dry, but it only needs a little). Serve immediately.

cabbage tagliatelle

1 pointed spring (sweetheart) cabbage, washed
extra vegan parmesan (bought or homemade, see p.263) or nutritional yeast, to serve (optional)

For the pesto sauce:
50g (2oz/⅓ cup) pine nuts
3–4 handfuls of fresh basil leaves, briefly washed and lightly patted dry
1 large or 2 small garlic cloves, peeled
1 tbsp nutritional yeast
½ tsp salt
4 tbsp extra virgin olive oil

I love using vegetable alternatives to make a classic pasta or grain dish – Cauliflower Couscous is an example (see p.94) and here is another. Pale green, firm and smooth pointed spring cabbage, sometimes called sweetheart cabbage, is one of my favourite vegetables; it's crisp but tender, with a fresh, delicate flavour. I love shredding and tossing it in olive oil, lemon juice and sea salt for a very quick salad side dish; cutting it into wedges and baking it in tomato sauce; and, perhaps most of all, cooking it in the style of pasta.

First, make the pesto. Toast the pine nuts in a dry frying pan over a low-medium heat, stirring until they begin to colour and smell toasty. Remove from the heat and transfer them to a food processor or a deep container for a stick (immersion) blender. Add the remaining pesto ingredients and whizz to a slightly chunky green pesto.

For the cabbage tagliatelle, halve the cabbage then slice across into thin tagliatelle-like strands.

Bring a 1-cm (½-in) depth of water to the boil in large saucepan. Add the cabbage, bring back to the boil, and cook for a few minutes until it is tender but still has a little 'bite' to it – 'al dente', you might say. Drain the cabbage, then return it to the still-hot pan. Stir in the pesto – as much as you want.

Serve the cabbage tagliatelle out onto warmed plates. You can offer some extra vegan parmesan or nutritional yeast to scatter on top, although I think this is just perfect exactly as it is.

note on pesto ...

You can use store-bought pesto for speed (good vegan ones are widely available), but as it's such a quick recipe in any case, sometimes it's really worth making your own pesto – you can whizz it up so quickly in a food processor and it's absolutely delicious. Do be generous with the fresh basil. I buy a whole plant from the supermarket and use it all to make this – well worth it. If there's any left over, it will keep for about a week in a covered container in the refrigerator – it's great on jacket potatoes and other veg too.

97

EASY AND DELICIOUS SOUPS

I love making soups – they're
so easy to do and so satisfying
to eat; and versatile too: lovely
to whet one's appetite at the start
of a meal, but also easy to make
into filling meals in their own
right. I sometimes think I could
live on soups – and, truth to tell,
there have been times in my life
when I pretty much have. Here
are a few of my favourites.

celeriac and parsley soup

This is a delicious soup, with a delicate, refreshing celery flavour and a light, but satisfying, texture.

Serves 4

1 tbsp olive oil

2 large onions, chopped

1 medium-large celeriac (celery root) (about 500–700g/1lb 2oz–1lb 9oz buying weight)

2l (70fl oz/8½ cups) water, or more as necessary

1 tbsp vegetable stock (bouillon) powder, or more as necessary

1–2 handfuls of flat-leaf parsley, chopped

juice of ½ lemon

sea salt and freshly ground black pepper, to taste

Heat the oil in a large heavy saucepan over a low heat, add the onion, cover and gently fry for about 5 minutes, until beginning to soften.

Meanwhile, prepare the celeriac (celery root): use a sharp knife to remove the outer skin, cutting it off fairly thickly, then cut the celeriac into chunky pieces about the size of small new potatoes.

Stir the celeriac chunks into the pan, add the water and stock (bouillon) powder and bring to the boil. Cover, reduce the heat and gently simmer for about 20 minutes, or until the celeriac is tender.

Add the parsley to the pan, then purée the soup in the pan with a hand-held (immersion) blender, or in a food processor – I like to purée it quite lightly, so that the celeriac and parsley remain distinct. You can adjust the thickness of the soup as necessary by adding a little more water, and perhaps a bit more bouillon powder, to allow for a slightly larger celeriac. You can never make too much of this soup in my experience!

Season with lemon juice and salt and pepper to taste, then serve.

carrot and lentil soup

Heat the oil in a large heavy saucepan over a low heat, add the onion, cover and fry gently without browning for 5 minutes, stirring occasionally.

Add the carrots, lentils, vegetable stock (bouillon) powder and 1 litre (35fl oz/4¼ cups) of the water and bring to the boil. Cover, reduce the heat and gently simmer for 20 minutes (if using a pressure cooker, cook for 5 minutes), until the carrot is tender and the lentils are pale.

Purée the soup in the pan with a hand-held (immersion) blender, or in a food processor, adding the remaining water as necessary to get the consistency you prefer (I like this soup quite thin). Stir in the lemon juice and add salt and pepper to taste.

Reheat gently and serve topped with some chopped fresh herbs.

variation

For a luxurious presentation, swirl some thick coconut cream over the top of each bowl along with some hot pepper sauce, before you add the chopped herbs.

note on equipment ...

A hand-held (immersion) blender is so useful for easy soup-making and many other recipes. I wouldn't be without mine.

This is a favourite soup; it tastes lovely and is very quick to make, especially if – like me – you use a pressure cooker, though this is by no means essential. You can vary the thickness to taste, and if you let it stand in the pan for a few hours it gets thicker: just add water to bring it back to the consistency you like.

Serves 6

1 tbsp olive oil
1 medium onion, chopped
750g (1lb 10 oz) carrots, roughly
    chopped into evenly sized pieces
125g (4½oz/⅔ cup) split red lentils
4 tsp vegetable stock (bouillon)
    powder
1–1.5l (35–52fl oz/4¼–6½ cups) water
juice of 1 lemon
sea salt and freshly ground black
    pepper
chopped fresh herbs,
    to garnish

image
p.100-101

instant miso broth

Crumble the wakame into a lidded mug or cup, add the miso and put the lid on.

When you're ready to eat, pour in some freshly boiled water and stir to combine. That's it!

variation

If you want something a bit more sustaining, you could fill another container with some perfectly cooked short grain brown rice and a small chopped spring onion (scallion), and take some gomasio (p.268) in a twist of foil to sprinkle on top. Don't forget to include a fork to eat it with, and you're good to go!

I absolutely love miso, and this instant broth is one of my favourite 'pick-me-ups'. It makes a great portable instant lunch. I like either barley or brown rice miso; they're pure, clean-tasting and delicious, and keep for ages in the refrigerator.

Serves 1

small piece of dried wakame sea
    vegetable (see p.15)
1 heaped tsp miso (see p.15)
freshly boiled water, to serve

polish borscht

Grate the peeled beetroots (beets) directly into a large heavy saucepan.

Pour over the boiling water and slowly bring to the boil, then reduce the heat and simmer for at least 10 minutes, until the beetroot begins to lose colour (if convenient, you can leave it much longer – up to 1 hour, until the beetroot looks 'bleached').

Remove from the heat and strain through a colander into another saucepan. Stir in the bouillon powder or stock cubes, making sure they are thoroughly dissolved, then add the garlic, lemon juice and sugar, salt and pepper to taste. Place the pan back over the heat to warm the soup through, then serve, garnished with dill, if wished.

This jewel-bright Polish *barszcz*, or borscht, is very easy to make and tastes as delicious as it looks. The longer you cook the beetroot (beets), the better the flavour. It's lovely served the Polish way, in large mugs, with small savoury pastries, or in bowls with a little feathery green dill sprinkled on top.

Serves 6–8

5–6 raw beetroot (beets), peeled
2l (70fl oz/8½ cups) boiling water
2–4 tsp vegetable bouillon powder
    or stock cubes
1–2 garlic cloves, crushed
juice of 1 lemon
sea salt and freshly ground black
    pepper, to taste
sugar, to taste
a few feathery dill fronds, to garnish
    (optional)

white bean soup with truffle oil

A quick and easy soup with a delicious flavour, especially if you swirl it with a little truffle oil, although it's delicious in any case!

Serves 4

2 tbsp olive oil
1 white onion, chopped
2 × 400g (14oz) cans cannellini beans, undrained
2 garlic cloves, crushed
500ml (17fl oz/2 cups) water
1 tsp vegetable stock (bouillon) powder
squeeze of fresh lemon juice
2 tbsp truffle oil
salt and freshly ground black pepper, to taste

Heat the olive oil in a large saucepan over a medium heat, add the onion and fry gently for about 5 minutes, stirring, until beginning to soften but not brown. Add the cannellini beans, along with their water, garlic, water and stock (bouillon) powder. Bring to the boil, then reduce the heat and leave to simmer gently for about 15 minutes, until the onion is tender.

Purée the soup in a blender or food processor, or use a stick blender, adding a little extra water to adjust the thickness of the soup if you wish. Add a dash of lemon juice and season with salt and pepper to taste.

Reheat gently, then serve in warmed bowls, with a little truffle oil swirled on top of each portion.

creamy cauliflower soup

Heat the olive oil in a large saucepan, add the cauliflower and fry over a fairly gentle heat for 5–10 minutes, until golden-brown in places. Add the water, bring to the boil, then reduce the heat and simmer gently for about 5 minutes, until the cauliflower is tender. Stir in the shelled hemp seeds and stock (bouillon) powder.

Process in a blender or with a hand-held stick (immersion) blender until the soup is completely smooth and creamy. You can add a little more water to thin it slightly, if necessary, then season to taste and serve with a garnish of chopped chives.

This is a useful soup to make when you've already cut two or three slices, or 'steaks', from a medium-sized cauliflower and are left with the remainder. There are actually plenty of delicious ways to use it as you'll find by looking through this book, but one of my favourites is this very quick creamy soup. It was inspired by the unusual one in *Vegan Keto*, by Liz MacDowell, which is thickened by nutritious shelled hemp seeds (you must make sure they're shelled ones).

Serves 4

2 tbsp olive oil
400g (14oz) cauliflower florets, roughly chopped
750ml (26fl oz/3¼ cups) water
60g (2oz/2 tbsp) shelled hemp seeds
1–2 tsp vegetable stock (bouillon) powder, or to taste
salt and freshly ground black pepper, to taste
a few chopped chives, to serve

shitake mushroom soup

Made from fresh shiitake mushrooms, this is a quick, beautifully clear and very tasty soup that is particularly lovely served before a meal as a starter or as an opener to an Asian-style meal.

Serves 3–4

2 tbsp toasted sesame oil
2 × 125g (4½oz) packs of fresh shiitake mushrooms, rinsed in cold water and patted dry with kitchen paper, then sliced
2–4 tsp vegetable stock (bouillon) powder, or to taste
500ml (17fl oz/2 cups) water
salt and freshly ground black pepper, to taste

Heat the oil in a saucepan over a low-medium heat, add the sliced mushrooms and fry for 2–3 minutes, until lightly cooked. Add the stock (bouillon) powder and water and bring to the boil, then reduce the heat and simmer for about 5 minutes.

Check the seasoning – it may not need any, as the stock powder is quite highly seasoned – and serve.

leek, carrot flower and dill soup

Put the leek and carrot into a saucepan with the water and stock (bouillon) powder and bring to the boil. Reduce the heat and simmer gently for 10–15 minutes until the vegetables are tender. Check the seasoning (the stock powder is already salty so you probably won't need to add more salt), then ladle into warmed bowls, scatter with the fresh herbs and serve.

This quick and easy soup is both refreshing and pretty with thinly sliced leeks and carrot 'flowers', in a clear broth. If you have a canelle knife (a little stainless-steel utensil with a V-shaped blade), you can run it down the sides of the carrot to form grooves before slicing, so that the slices look like flowers – it gives a very pretty effect, but even without this, it's a lovely soup.

Serves 4–6

1 leek, about 170g (6oz), trimmed and
    thinly sliced
1 medium carrot, about 125g (4½oz),
    peeled and sliced as described
    above
1.5l (52fl oz/6½ cups) water
1–1½ tbsp vegan stock (bouillon)
    powder, or to taste
salt and freshly ground black pepper,
    to taste
1–2 tbsp fresh dill or chopped chives

meals in moments

almost instant

Pitta bread pizza: spread a pitta bread or wrap with tomato passata from a jar, or simply chopped tomatoes. Top with other favourite things, such as sliced baby mushrooms, artichoke hearts from a jar, asparagus spears and some 'Melting Cheese' (p.262), then grill (broil).

'Melting Cheese' on toast: Exactly what it says it is: a piece of toast – I like white sourdough bloomer the best – topped with 'Melting Cheese' (p.262) and put under the grill (broiler) until bubbly and golden brown. It's really fast if you plan slightly ahead to the extent of having

some of the 'cheese' mixture in the refrigerator or freezer.

Mushrooms on sourdough toast (see p.54): if you can get some 'wild' mushrooms, so much the better; delicious, especially when you cook the mushrooms and spread the toast with homemade vegan butter (see p.266). Top with a little chopped parsley.

Chilli beans with avocado and greens: exactly what it says. Warm through some canned chilli beans in sauce and serve with sliced avocado and your favourite quick-cook green vegetable. I like broccoli spears or leaf spinach.

fast to prepare, but take about 30 minutes to cook

Roasted potato wedges (p.118): with baked beans, or (if you have more time) Beany Stew (p.118), rocket (arugula) and avocado salad, or with Cheese Sauce (p.261).

Quick Dal (p.135): with rice or Cauliflower Couscous (p.94); mango chutney or a raw Indian chutney made by mixing together chopped raw tomato, onion and some sprigs of coriander (cilantro); and poppadums.

Jacket Potatoes (p.84): with any of the serving suggestions given, especially vegan butter and grated hard vegan cheese; hummus, or salad

leaves. These do take a bit longer than 30 minutes to cook (about 1 hour), but are so easy I'm including them. You can speed them up (to 30–40 minutes) if you halve the potatoes lengthways before cooking. Brush the cut surface with a little olive oil and bake on a roasting tin (pan) – this way, they'll also have a lovely crisp side, like a roast potato.

Fast and Easy Roasted Summer Vegetables (p.82): One of my absolute favourite quick meals. Use quick-to prepare vegetables, as suggested in the recipe, pop them into the

oven and the meal is practically ready by the time you've laid the table!

Roasted Winter Vegetables (p.81): these are very fast too. Pop them into the oven and, while they're cooking, prepare some Hummus (p.64) and some tenderstem broccoli, which cooks quickly in a saucepan with a little boiling water when the roasted veg are almost done.

Grilled 'Halloumi' Platter (p.74): a tasty quick dish to make if you like firm tofu, cooked in the style of halloumi cheese, and served with Mediterranean accompaniments – minty tzatziki, black olives, a simple tomato salad and toasted pitta bread.

Crisp Oven-baked Sesame Aubergine Fritters (p.86): lovely served with quick-cooked oven French fries if you like them, a handful of rocket (arugula) leaves and Quick Creamy Caper Sauce (p.156), which you can make while they're in the oven.

Instant Macaroni Cheese (p.124): make up the dry instant 'cheese' sauce mix and keep it in your storecupboard or fridge, and you can whip up this delicious dish in moments.

Broccoli and Coconut Curry (p.136): with quickly cooked basmati rice; delicious garnished with sliced tomato and chopped fresh coriander (cilantro).

Spaghetti Bolognese (p.121)

Creamy Leek Risotto (p.120)

light bites and lunches

111

midweek
mains

One of the hardest things about making the transition to veganism can be missing out on the foods that you've always turned to for comfort – those dishes that lift your mood, take you back to your childhood and make everything seem ok again. That doesn't have to be the case though and each of the recipes on the following pages is a hug on a plate that will leave you calm, sated and content.

'fish' cakes

If you're missing a taste of the sea, do try these – they're amazing. You can easily buy canned jackfruit in supermarkets and online and it has the same flaky texture as fish. Delicious with Garlic Tofu Mayonnaise (see p.256) and chips.

Makes 8

1 × 400g (14oz) can jackfruit in water or brine
50g (2oz) soft white bread, crusts removed
25g (1oz) red onion
40g (1½oz) celery
handful of flat-leaf parsley
1 sheet nori seaweed, roughly torn
1 tbsp freshly squeezed lemon juice
1 tsp Dijon mustard
2 tsp white wine vinegar or cider vinegar
dried panko breadcrumbs, for coating
4–5 tbsp olive oil
salt and freshly ground black pepper, to taste

Drain the jackfruit and pat dry on paper towels.

Put the bread, onion, celery and parsley into a food processor and process until chopped. Add the jackfruit, nori, lemon juice, mustard and vinegar, and process again until everything is roughly chopped and beginning to hold together. Season with salt and pepper; not too much salt as the jackfruit may already be a little salty. Form the mixture into 8 cakes.

Place the breadcrumbs in a bowl. Roll the cakes in the crumbs, pressing them gently so that they hold together.

Heat enough oil for shallow frying in a frying pan over a medium heat. Fry the cakes for 2–3 minutes on each side, until crisp and golden brown on both sides, then remove to drain on paper towels.

sausage and mash

Place the potatoes in a large saucepan and cover with cold water. Bring to the boil over a medium heat, then reduce to a simmer and leave to cook until just tender, 15–20 minutes.

Meanwhile, make the sausages. Put the walnuts, bread and onion into a food processor and pulse briefly to break them down a bit, then add the paprika and garlic powder and process in bursts, until you have a fairly smooth mixture that holds together. Season with salt and pepper to taste. Form the mixture by hand into 8 sausages.

Heat enough olive oil for shallow frying in a frying pan (skillet) over a medium heat and fry the sausages until lightly browned and crisp, 7–10 minutes. They need to be flattened slightly as you cook them and turned frequently so that they get nicely crisp all over.

Once the potatoes are tender, drain through a colander and leave to steam dry for a couple of minutes. Once dry, return the potatoes to the pan with the butter and milk, then cover with a lid and leave for a couple of minutes until the butter has melted. Mash the potatoes until smooth and creamy, then season to taste.

Place a generous spoonful of mash in the centre of four plates, then divide the sausuages between the plates and spoon over the onion gravy. Serve hot.

There are a wide range of vegan sausages available to buy, but it's also quick and easy to make your own and these are delicious – I love them! Try them as part of a cooked vegan breakfast, as hot dogs, or fried crisp and dipped in a little mustard, or, as here, with creamy mashed potato and moreish onion gravy.

Serves 4

200g (7oz/1½ cups) walnut halves
160g (5¾oz) bread
2 red onions, roughly chopped
1 tsp smoked paprika
2 tsp garlic powder or granules
sea salt and freshly ground black pepper
2–4 tbsp olive oil, for frying
Red Onion Gravy (see p.253), to serve

For the mashed potatoes:
1kg/2lb 4oz floury potatoes, peeled and cut into 2.5cm/1in chunks
25g/1oz Vegan Butter (see p.266) or vegan spread
2 tbsp plant milk of choice
salt and freshly ground black pepper, to taste

spiced bean stew with rosemary potato wedges

My daughter Meg makes this very fast, tasty, after-work recipe, which everyone enjoys. It is nice served with potato wedges, as here, or with jacket potatoes or rice. For a really easy meal, serve with oven fries.

Serves 6

1 tsp garam masala
1 tsp ground cumin
1 tsp ground coriander
1 tbsp olive oil
1 onion, chopped
2 garlic cloves, crushed
1 red chilli, deseeded and chopped
1 × 400g (14oz) can kidney beans, drained and rinsed
1 × 400g (14oz) can borlotti beans, drained and rinsed
1 × 400g (14oz) can adzuki beans, drained and rinsed
2 × 400g (14oz) cans chopped tomatoes
1 × 250g (7oz) pack puy lentils
1 tbsp vegan stock (bouillon) powder (with salt)
juice of 1 lemon
sea salt and freshly ground black pepper, to taste

For the potato wedges:
6 baking potatoes
drizzle of olive oil
1 sprig fresh rosemary, leaves chopped, or 1 tbsp dried rosemary

Preheat the oven to 200°C/400°F/gas mark 6.

Dry fry the garam masala, ground cumin, ground coriander in a large saucepan over a high heat for a few minutes to release their aromas. Pour in the olive oil, add the onion and fry until the onion is soft, then add the garlic and chilli and fry for a further 2 minutes.

Reduce the heat, add the beans, chopped tomatoes, lentils and stock (bouillon) powder and cook gently for about 15 minutes, stirring occasionally. Add the lemon juice to brighten the flavour and season with salt and pepper.

Meanwhile, cut the potatoes in half lengthways, then slice each half into thirds or quarters to make thin wedges. Put the wedges into a large bowl, drizzle with olive oil and scatter with the fresh or dried rosemary. Toss the wedges until well coated, then place in a single layer on a baking sheet. Bake for 20–30 minutes, until crispy on the outside and soft in the middle.

Serve the beany stew with the potato wedges.

creamy leek risotto

This risotto is creamy and delicious and can be made from start to finish in 35 minutes, so it's perfect for a weekday supper.

Serves 4

Heat 50g (2oz/3½ tbsp) of the butter and the olive oil in a large saucepan with a lid over a medium heat. Add the garlic and leeks, stir to coat in the butter, then cover and cook over a gentle heat for about 10 minutes.

Add the rice, increase the heat and cook, stirring, for 1–2 minutes until the rice looks slightly translucent. Pour in the wine or vermouth and stir for 1–2 minutes, until it has been absorbed, then add a ladleful of hot stock (bouillon) and a good pinch of salt. Reduce the heat to a simmer and keep adding ladlefuls of stock, stirring and allowing each ladleful to be absorbed before adding the next, until the rice is soft but with a slight bite, about 20 minutes. If you run out of stock before the rice is cooked, just add a little boiling water.

Remove the pan from the heat and gently stir in the remaining vegan butter, then cover and let stand for 2 minutes, until the rice has absorbed the butter and become rich and creamy. Divide the risotto among serving bowls, scatter over the almonds and thyme leaves, then serve immediately.

75g (2½oz/⅓ cup) Vegan Butter (see p.266) or vegan spread
1 tbsp olive oil
2 garlic cloves, finely chopped
3 large leeks (about 500g/1lb 2oz), washed, trimmed and thinly sliced
400g (14oz/2 cups) risotto rice
100ml (3½fl oz/scant ½ cup) dry white wine or vermouth
1l (35fl oz/4¼ cups) hot vegan vegetable stock (bouillon)
sea salt and freshly ground black pepper, to taste

To serve:
50g (2oz/generous ½ cup) flaked (slivered) almonds, toasted
few sprigs fresh thyme leaves, chopped

spaghetti bolognese

This is quick to make from storecupboard ingredients. It's lovely topped with vegan parmesan-style cheese, if you can find any, or it's quick and easy to make your own (see p.263).

Start by making the sauce: heat the olive oil in a saucepan over a low-medium heat, add the onions and cook gently for 5 minutes without browning. Add the garlic, celery and carrots and simmer, covered with a lid, for 15 minutes until the vegetables are tender.

Stir in the chopped tomatoes and lentils, along with enough of the reserved liquid to form a thick consistency. Simmer for 5–10 minutes, adding more liquid if necessary, until the lentils are well heated through. Season to taste with salt and pepper.

Meanwhile, bring a saucepan of water to the boil, add the spaghetti and simmer for about 10 minutes, until just tender. Drain, then return the spaghetti to the pan, stir through the olive oil and season with salt and pepper.

Place the spaghetti on a warmed serving dish and pour the sauce on top. Serve immediately, topped with grated vegan hard cheese.

Serves 4

225–350g (8–12oz) spaghetti
2 tbsp olive oil
salt and freshly ground black pepper, to taste
vegan hard cheese, grated, or 'Parmesan' (see p.263), to serve

For the sauce:
2 tbsp olive oil
2 onions, chopped
2 garlic cloves, crushed
2 celery sticks, chopped
2 carrots, coarsely grated
2 × 400g (14oz) cans green lentils, drained, liquid reserved
1 × 400g (14oz) can chopped tomatoes
salt and freshly ground black pepper, to taste

artichoke and asparagus paella

Lovely to look at, full of flavour and very quick and easy to make, this can also be made in advance, covered, and gently reheated – perfect for relaxed entertaining. I don't think it needs any accompaniment, except perhaps for a nice glass of wine.

Serves 4

Heat the olive oil in a large heavy saucepan, frying pan or paella pan over a low-medium heat, add the onion and garlic, and fry gently for 5 minutes.

Add the rice to the pan, stirring gently for a few seconds until all the grains are coated with oil, then add the tomatoes and stock (bouillon) and bring to the boil. Reduce to a simmer and cook gently for 10 minutes, stirring from time to time.

Add the peppers, leek and asparagus and cook for a further 10 minutes, until the vegetables are tender.

Meanwhile, drain the artichoke hearts in a sieve (fine-mesh strainer) and rinse under some just boiled water from the kettle. Gently stir them into the paella.

Stir in a little lemon juice to taste and season as necessary with salt and pepper. Serve scattered with the fresh chopped parsley.

1 tbsp olive oil

1 onion, chopped

1 garlic clove, crushed

300g (10½oz/generous 1½ cups) paella rice

1 × 400g (14oz) can chopped tomatoes

900ml (31fl oz/scant 4 cups) vegetable stock (bouillon)

1 red (bell) pepper, trimmed, deseeded and chopped

1 yellow (bell) pepper, trimmed, deseeded and chopped

1 leek, trimmed and cut into 2cm (¾in) pieces

100g (3½oz) thin asparagus spears, trimmed as necessary

½–1 tsp dried chilli flakes, to taste

1 × 285g (10oz) jar artichoke hearts in oil, drained

juice of 1 lemon, or to taste

handful of fresh flat-leaf parsley, chopped

salt and freshly ground black pepper, to taste

instant macaroni cheese

This is my version of a wonderful recipe that my daughter Kate found on one of her favourite websites, *Bit of the Good Stuff*. You make up a batch of dry mix ready for use, then it only takes a few minutes to whizz up a delicious macaroni cheese that all the family will love. One batch of the dry mix will serve a family of four, or can be divided into four individual serving portions, so once the ingredients have been combined, you can weigh the mixture, take a note of the amount, then portion out as needed.

To make the dry mix, combine all the ingredients in a food processor and process to a powder. If not using immediately, store in an airtight container in the refrigerator for up to 6 weeks.

Bring a large saucepan of water to the boil and cook the pasta according to the packet instructions. Drain and set aside.

Meanwhile, make the sauce. Put the dry mix into a saucepan set over a low-medium heat and whisk in your chosen liquid. Cook, stirring constantly, for 1–2 minutes or until it has thickened. Thin with a bit more liquid, if you like, then taste and season as necessary.

Mix the sauce and pasta together. You can serve it immediately or bake it, if you wish.

If baking, preheat the oven to 180°C/350°F/gas mark 4. Put the macaroni cheese mixture into a shallow ovenproof dish, scatter with breadcrumbs and bake for 20–30 minutes, until golden brown and crisp.

Serve with cooked peas or salad, as you wish.

variation

Cauliflower or Broccoli Bake: instead of the macaroni, use 1 medium cauliflower or 2 heads of broccoli, broken into florets and cooked in boiling water for a few minutes until tender. Drain and mix with the sauce, along with 200–250g (7–9oz) cherry tomatoes. Then bake as described above.

Serves 4

For the 'instant dry mix' (makes enough for 4 servings):
110g (4oz/generous ¾ cup) cashews
35g (1¼oz/generous ½ cup) nutritional yeast
20g (¾oz/3 heaped tbsp) rolled oats
25g (1oz/3 tbsp) tapioca flour
2½ tsp brown sugar
1 tbsp paprika
1½ tsp mustard powder
1½ tsp onion powder
¾ tsp salt

To finish:
1 x recipe quantity 'instant dry mix' (above)
1l (35fl oz/4¼ cups) plant milk or water (or half and half)
400g (14oz/4½ cups) macaroni
handful of breadcrumbs mixed with 1 tbsp olive oil, for topping (if baking)
salt and freshly ground black pepper, to taste
cooked peas or salad, to serve

bean lasagne

Preheat the oven to 200°C/400°F/gas mark 6. Grease a shallow baking dish, about 23 × 33cm (9 × 13in).

Bring a large saucepan of salted water to the boil and cook the lasagne sheets until just tender. Drain, then drape the pieces over the edges of the colander to prevent them from sticking together.

Heat the oil in a large saucepan over a medium heat, add the onions and fry for 10 minutes, then add the kidney beans, mashing them as you do so. Add the chopped tomatoes, tomato purée (paste), cinnamon and wine and mix well. Season to taste.

Place a layer of the lasagne sheets in the baking dish and top with half of the red bean mixture and a quarter of the cheese sauce. Repeat to make a second layer of lasagne sheets, red beans and cheesy sauce, then top with a final layer of lasagne and the remaining cheesy sauce. Bake for 45 minutes.

I like to use green spinach lasagne, but do ensure the lasagne sheets are egg-free. If you prefer to use 'no cook' fresh lasagne, add an extra 150ml (5fl oz/⅔ cup) of the 'Cheese Sauce'.

Serves 4

2 tbsp olive oil, plus extra for greasing
170g (6oz) dried vegan lasagne sheets
2 onions, chopped
2 × 400g (14oz) cans red kidney beans, drained
1 × 225g (8oz) can chopped tomatoes
2 tbsp tomato purée (paste)
1 tsp ground cinnamon
2 tbsp red wine
1¼ x recipe quantity 'Cheese Sauce' (see p.261) (about 750ml/ 25fl oz/3¼ cups)
salt and freshly ground black pepper, to taste

easy bean chilli

Heat the oil in a large saucepan over a low heat, add the onion and red (bell) pepper and cook gently for about 15 minutes, until starting to become tender. Add the garlic, chopped tomatoes, kidney beans and chilli powder and season with salt and pepper to taste. Cook, stirring from time to time, for a further 10 minutes or until all the vegetables are tender.

Serve with cooked rice or crusty bread, garnished with some chopped coriander (cilantro) or parsley.

Serves 2

1 tbsp olive oil
1 onion, chopped
1 red (bell) pepper, deseeded and chopped
1 garlic clove, crushed
1 × 400g (14oz) can chopped tomatoes
1 × 400g (14oz) can red kidney beans, drained
1 pinch chilli powder
salt and freshly ground black pepper, to taste
chopped fresh coriander (cilantro) or parsley, to garnish
cooked rice or crusty bread, to serve

Depending on where in the world you live, the vegan revolution might not quite have made it to your local takeaway. Fear not though, because, from fish and chips to burgers, you can easily create versions of your favourite takeaway classics at home that, on top of being fully vegan, have the additional benefits of being both healthier and kinder on the pocket than the traditional versions.

'tofish' and chips

This is one of my husband's favourite recipes. To make it, you need a fairly firm tofu as well as a flavoursome nori – that pressed seaweed that looks like sheets of carbon paper and should say 'toasted and ready to use', or 'roasted' on the packet. If you're serving chips, start cooking them before you start frying the tofu, so that everything is ready together.

Drain the tofu and blot dry on paper towels, then slice into 9 pieces. Cut the nori into strips the same width as the tofu pieces – you should get 3 strips out of each piece of nori.

Brush the tofu with the soy sauce, then wrap each piece in a strip of nori.

To make the batter, combine the flour, baking powder and salt in a large bowl, then stir in enough sparkling water to make a thick, coating batter.

Heat a 1cm (½in) depth of oil in a heavy saucepan or deep frying pan over a medium-high heat. Dip each piece of wrapped tofu in the batter, then carefully transfer it to the hot oil and fry for about 2–3 minutes on each side until they are a lovely golden brown, puffed-up and crunchy – they are lovely when they are crisp and dark golden brown in colour.

Remove with a slotted spoon to drain on paper towels, then transfer to the oven while you cook the remainder. Serve warm, with chips and tartare sauce alongside.

Serves 2–3

1 × 280g (10oz) packet firm tofu
3 nori sheets
2–3 tbsp shoyu (Japanese) soy sauce
mild olive oil, for-deep-frying
chips and vegan tartare sauce
    (see p.258), to serve (optional)

For the batter:
100g (3½oz/¾ cup) plain (all-purpose)
    flour
1 tsp baking powder
½ tsp salt
about 150ml (5fl oz/⅔ cup) sparkling
    water

quesadillas

Heat 1 tbsp of the olive oil in a large saucepan over a medium heat, add the onion and peppers and fry for about 10 minutes, stirring from time to time, until tender.

Add the mushrooms, spinach, beans, spices and herbs, and cook, stirring, for 2–3 minutes, then remove from the heat. Season with salt and set aside.

Thinly coat a large, preferably non-stick, frying pan (skillet) with a little of the remaining olive oil and set over a medium heat. Place a tortilla in the pan and sprinkle over one-eighth of the cheese to cover the tortilla. Spread one-eighth of the filling mixture over half of the tortilla, then top with some of the avocado and spring onion. Fold over the other side of the tortilla to enclose the filling. Fry for about 3 minutes, pressing down on the top of the tortilla to help seal the edges with the melted cheese, until the tortilla is crispy and golden brown, then flip it over and fry the other side for a further 3 minutes. Remove from the pan and cut it in half. Keep the quesadilla warm in a cool oven while you repeat with the remaining tortillas and the rest of the mixture.

Serve warm, with soured cream if you like.

Serves 4–6

2 tbsp olive oil
1 red onion, thinly sliced
1 red (bell) pepper, halved, deseeded and thinly sliced
1 yellow (bell) pepper, halved, deseeded and thinly sliced
200g (7oz) mushrooms, sliced
100g (3½oz) baby spinach
1 × 400g (14oz) can red kidney beans or other canned beans of your choice, drained
1 tsp each chilli powder, cumin and dried oregano (or other spices, to taste)
8 medium tortillas
1 x recipe quantity Melting 'Cheese' (see p.262) or store-bought vegan mozzarella-style cheese
1 avocado, peeled, pitted and sliced
2 spring onions (scallions), chopped
salt, to taste
Soured Vegan Cream (see p.267), to serve (optional)

curried chickpea cakes

Serves 2

3 tbsp olive oil
1 red onion, finely chopped
2–3 tsp vegan korma curry paste,
    or to taste
1 garlic clove, crushed
1 × 400g (14oz) can chickpeas
    (garbanzo beans), drained (reserve
    the liquid for aquafaba – see p.13)
salt, to taste
30g (1oz/¾ cup) panko breadcrumbs,
    for coating

These make a great spicy side dish to serve with a curry or I also love them on their own. They're ideal to make if you find yourself in the situation of having chickpeas (garbanzo beans) to use up, because you've used their liquid (known in the vegan world as 'aquafaba') to whisk up in place of egg white in meringues (see also p.244, it's strange but true – you may find yourself looking for ways to use up spare chickpeas!).

They're lovely served warm or cold, with mango chutney, white basmati rice and a quickly cooked green vegetable, such as spinach or broccoli. If you're serving these with rice, get it on to cook before you start – it cooks quickly, but can always wait, off the heat, once done.

Heat 1 tbsp of the olive oil in a medium saucepan over a low-medium heat, add the onion and curry paste and fry for 7–10 minutes until the onion is tender. Remove from the heat, add the garlic and chickpeas (garbanzo beans) and roughly mash until combined. Add salt, to taste.

Gently but firmly form the mixture into 2 flat rounds, so that they hold together.

Place the breadcrumbs in a bowl and press the patties into the breadcrumbs until coated on both sides.

Heat the remaining 2 tbsp of olive oil in a frying pan over a medium heat and fry the cakes for about 2 minutes on each side until crisp and golden brown. Remove to drain on paper towels.

*image
p.132*

spicy bean burgers

It's really easy to make your own spicy bean burgers, and you can adjust the 'heat' according to your taste.

Serves 4

Heat 1 tbsp of the olive oil in a medium saucepan over a low-medium heat, add the onion and fry for 7–10 minutes until tender. Add the ground cumin and smoked paprika and stir for a few seconds over the heat to cook briefly. Transfer the mixture to a food processor, add the beans, cherry tomatoes and soft breadcrumbs, then process until well combined. Taste and add a little salt if necessary.

Gently but firmly form the mixture into 4 flat rounds, so that they hold together. Place the panko breadcrumbs in a bowl and press the patties into the breadcrumbs until coated on both sides.

Heat the remaining 2 tbsp of olive oil in a frying pan (skillet) over a medium heat and fry the burgers for about 2 minutes on each side until crisp and golden brown, adding more oil to the pan if necessary. Remove to drain on paper towels.

Serve just as they are, with salad and perhaps some chips (fries) and homemade mayo (p.258), or in a bun with lettuce and tomatoes.

3 tbsp olive oil
1 red onion, finely chopped
1 tsp ground cumin
½ tsp smoked paprika
1 × 400g (14oz) can red kidney beans, drained (reserve the liquid for aquafaba – see p.13)
80g (3oz) cherry tomatoes, stems removed
50g (2oz/1 cup) soft white breadcrumbs (2 slices of a sliced loaf; I prefer sourdough)
salt, to taste
30g (1oz/¾ cup) panko breadcrumbs, for coating

image p.133

quick nut burgers

2 tbsp olive oil

2 onions, finely chopped

100g (3½oz/¾ cup) walnuts

100g (3½oz/¾ cup) cashews

100g (3½oz/¾ cup) almonds

100g (3½oz) sliced white or wholemeal
    bread, roughly torn

1 tsp dried mixed herbs or 'herbes de
    Provence'

3 tbsp shoyu (Japanese) or other soy
    sauce

3–4 tbsp olive oil, for frying

sea salt and freshly ground black
    pepper, to taste

These are ultra-quick to whizz up if you've got a food processor. I particularly like using shoyu (Japanese) soy sauce for this recipe, as it is traditionally made, pure and delicious, but other types can also be used. These are delicious served warm with quick steamed broccoli (see p.173) and perhaps some vegan gravy. Alternatively, serve them cold, with pickles and chutney. The Red Pepper Sauce (p.254) or Tomato Sauce (p.164) is also great with them. If you make double the recipe, the other half can be used to make a nut roast.

Heat the oil in a large saucepan over a low-medium heat, add the onions and fry for about 10 minutes until tender.

Put the onions into a food processor along with the nuts, bread, herbs and soy sauce and process until combined. Season with salt and pepper – it won't need much salt as the soy sauce is already salty.

Form the mixture into 10 flat rounds.

Heat the oil in a frying pan over a medium heat and fry the burgers for 3–5 minutes on each side until well browned, turning them carefully. Remove to drain on paper towels.

A delicately spiced curry is a thing of a beauty, but is all too often banished to the typical Friday night takeaway. But with a little know-how (and a couple of jars of ready-made vegan curry paste), you can have a deliciously fragrant curry on the table in the time it takes to cook the rice, making it the perfect mid-week pick-me-up. The recipes on the following pages will help you spice up your life whatever the occasion, and a full menu for a sumptuous (and easy!) Indian feast will make midweek entertaining a doddle.

quick dal

Fill a large saucepan with 1.5l (52fl oz/6½ cups) water, add the lentils, chopped chillies and turmeric and bring to the boil. Cook for 20 minutes, or until the lentils are tender and pale in colour, adding a little more water if they begin to stick towards the end of the cooking time.

Meanwhile, in a separate saucepan, melt the butter or margarine over a low-medium heat, add the onions and fry for about 10 minutes until golden brown. Add the garlic, cumin and ginger, and fry for a few minutes longer.

Add the onion and spice mixture to the lentils, along with the chopped tomatoes, and cook for a further 5–10 minutes, until the tomatoes are cooked through.

Serve, scattered with fresh coriander (cilantro).

This is one of my favourite really quick meals. Okay, you do have to wait for the lentils to soften, but that only takes about 20 minutes; in around 30 minutes, you have a filling, tasty meal. It's lovely with some crunchy poppadums and maybe some mango chutney on the side. If there is any left over, it makes nice fritters, which are very easy to make, simply mixed with some soft breadcrumbs and fried in oil.

Serves 4

450g (1lb/2½ cups) dried red lentils
1–2 red chillies, or to taste, chopped
½ tsp ground turmeric
25g (1oz/scant 2 tbsp) vegan butter or margarine
2 onions, sliced
4 garlic cloves, chopped
½ tsp cumin seeds
2cm (½in) piece of fresh root ginger, grated
2 tomatoes, chopped
fresh coriander (cilantro), chopped, to garnish

broccoli and coconut curry

This is so quick and easy to make and absolutely delicious. If you have an onion, a can of coconut milk and some rice in the cupboard, and some vegan curry paste in the fridge, you only need to buy a couple of fresh ingredients and you've got your meal.

Bring a shallow saucepan of water to the boil, add the broccoli and boil for about 5 minutes, or until it is tender to the point of a knife. Drain and set aside.

Meanwhile, heat the olive oil in a separate saucepan over a low heat. Add the onion and garlic and fry gently for 7–10 minutes, until tender.

Stir in the curry paste and coconut milk and gently heat through, then stir in the broccoli. Reheat gently if necessary, and season with salt to taste.

Serve with rice, scattered with the fresh coriander (cilantro) and garnished with the tomato slices.

note on curry paste ...

I used to make my own curry mixtures with fresh spices, but I have recently started to save time by using ready-made curry pastes. You can buy them from any supermarket and, really, they are just as good!

Serves 4

1 large or 2 small heads of broccoli (about 500g/1lb 2oz), trimmed and cut into bite-size pieces
1 tbsp olive oil
1 medium white onion, chopped
2 garlic cloves, crushed
1 tbsp curry paste (see note)
1 × 400g (14oz) can full-fat coconut milk salt, to taste

To serve:
cooked basmati rice
few sprigs fresh coriander (cilantro), roughly chopped or snipped
1 firm beefsteak tomato, sliced

thai green curry

Heat the oil in a large saucepan or wok over a medium heat, add the onion and fry for 5 minutes until beginning to soften. Stir in the garlic and 2 tbsp curry paste (you can always add more later, to taste, if necessary) and cook for 1–2 minutes, then add the broccoli and pak choi and stir to coat in the paste. Stir in the coconut milk, half cover with a lid, then leave to cook gently for about 15 minutes, stirring from time to time, until the vegetables are tender. Finally, stir in lime juice, salt and pepper, to taste.

Serve with rice, garnished with the chopped coriander (cilantro) and cashews.

Jars of both green and red vegan Thai curry pastes are widely available – I've used the green here for this fast and tasty curry. You can vary the recipe by using the red curry paste and including some different vegetables, such as carrot sticks, slices of red (bell) pepper and baby mushrooms, for a change.

Serves 3–4

2 tbsp coconut oil, melted, sesame oil or mild olive oil

1 red onion, sliced

2 garlic cloves, crushed

2–3 tbsp green vegan curry paste

1 large head of broccoli, trimmed and cut into bite-size pieces

2 pak choi, quartered then roughly chopped

1 × 400g (14oz) can coconut milk

juice of ½–1 lime

salt and freshly ground black pepper, to taste

handful of fresh coriander (cilantro), chopped, to garnish

handful of roasted cashews, to garnish

cooked basmati rice, to serve

easy indian feast

SERVES 4

This is a wonderful feast of flavours and it's easy to put together. You could choose just one or two of the dishes, or make them all, for an easy and delicious Indian-inspired feast. I like to serve it with some poppadums and mango chutney.

Check beforehand that you have the right spices for the Bombay potatoes, as they make all the difference to this simple dish. Stock up, then keep them handy for another time – if you're anything like me, this will become a favourite and you'll want to make it again!

Start by making the dal, then the Bombay potatoes and the rice. While they're cooking, prepare the fresh tomato and onion salad and the minty yogurt sauce. At the last minute, cook some spinach: I buy a bag of ready-washed leaf spinach (always organic, if possible), either microwave (make a few holes in the bag with a sharp knife, then microwave it for a few seconds until the leaves are just wilted) or steam, and turn them onto a warmed dish for serving.

simple dal (p.141)

bombay potatoes (p.141)

easy pilau rice (p.142)

fresh tomato and onion salad (p.143)

minty yogurt sauce (p.143)

red onion bhajis (p.142)

steamed spinach

poppadums

mango chutney

simple dal

This is such an easy recipe – it's great as a starter, but also filling enough to be a meal in its own right, perhaps with some poppadums or nan bread and some sliced tomato with chopped fresh coriander (cilantro).

Serves 4

200g (7oz/generous 1 cup) split red lentils
800ml (27fl oz/scant 3½ cups) water
2 garlic cloves, thinly sliced
1 tsp black or brown mustard seeds
3–4 tsp curry paste
juice of ½ lemon
salt, to taste
handful chopped fresh coriander (cilantro),
    to garnish

Combine the lentils, water, garlic and mustard seeds in a deep saucepan and bring to the boil. Simmer for 15–20 minutes, until the lentils are tender and golden.

Stir in the curry paste and lemon juice and add salt to taste.

Serve, scattered with chopped fresh coriander (cilantro).

bombay potatoes

This is delicious as a side dish to serve with other spicy dishes. If there's any left over, it makes a good snack, reheated, perhaps with a little mango chutney.

Serves 4

3 tbsp olive oil
½ tsp brown mustard seeds and ¼ tsp yellow
    mustard seeds (or use ¾ tsp of one or the
    other)
¼ tsp ground cumin
½ tsp ground turmeric
¼ tsp ground coriander
¼ tsp chilli powder
500g (1lb 2oz) potatoes, peeled and cut into
    bite-size pieces if large
½ tsp salt
100ml (3½fl oz/scant ½ cup) water
small handful roughly chopped fresh coriander
    (cilantro), to garnish

Heat the oil in a medium saucepan with a lid over a medium heat, add the mustard seeds and fry until they start to pop and jump around, then stir in the remaining spices. Add the potatoes, stir for a moment to coat with the oil and spices, then add the salt and water. Bring to the boil, cover and cook for 15 minutes or until all the water has evaporated and the potatoes are beginning to fry in the oil.

Check the seasoning and serve scattered with some roughly chopped coriander (cilantro).

easy pilau rice

Make perfect rice every time with this easy recipe!

Serves 4

300g (10½oz/scant 1¾ cups) white basmati rice
generous knob of homemade Vegan Butter
    (see p.266) or vegan spread
3 cardamom pods, crushed
1 cinnamon stick, broken
salt and freshly ground black pepper, to taste

Half-fill a large saucepan (with a lid) with water and bring to the boil. Put the rice into a sieve (strainer), rinse quickly under running cold water, then tip the rice into the saucepan. Bring back to the boil and simmer for 7 minutes. For perfect rice, the timing is important. Drain and shake off excess water, but don't let the rice get too dry.

Rinse and quickly dry the saucepan and put it back on the heat, or use a second saucepan. Add the vegan butter and the spices and cook over a gentle heat, stirring, for 1–2 minutes, then stir in the drained rice. Cover with the lid and cook over a very gentle heat for 30 minutes.

Remove from the heat and let stand for 1–2 minutes before serving, if you have the time.

red onion bhajis

These are easy to make and delicious with curry.

Serves 4

olive oil, for deep frying
125g (4½oz/1 cup) chickpea (gram) flour
2 tsp ground coriander
1 tsp ground cumin
1 pinch cayenne pepper
1 tsp salt
150ml (5fl oz/⅔ cup) warm water
1 red onion, finely sliced

Heat a 3cm (1in) depth of oil in a large deep frying pan, saucepan or deep-fat fryer over a medium-high heat.

Meanwhile, sift the chickpea (gram) flour into a bowl with the spices and salt, then pour in the water and mix to a batter.

Stir the sliced onions into the batter. Carefully lower spoonfuls of the mixture into the hot oil and fry for about 5 minutes, or until the batter is really crisp and the onions are tender. Don't overcrowd the pan – cook them in batches. Remove with a slotted spoon to drain on paper towels and keep warm, uncovered, while you cook the rest.

Serve immediately.

fresh tomato and onion salad

This is a refreshing side dish to serve with curry, as much a kind of raw 'chutney' as a 'salad'.

Serves 4

2–3 firm tomatoes, chopped
1 small onion, finely sliced or chopped
salt, to taste

Just mix all the ingredients together and put into a small bowl for people to help themselves.

minty yogurt sauce

When choosing a plain vegan yogurt look for one with the fewest ingredients. I also like to vary the kinds of milk and yogurt I used, rather than depending on one, such as soya: but my main rule of thumb is to choose the most natural one I can, with the fewest ingredients and no unpronounceable additives!

Serves 4

4 heaped tbsp plain vegan yogurt
1 tbsp chopped fresh mint
salt, to taste

Just mix the yogurt and mint together in a small bowl, season with a little salt, and serve.

meg's noodle stir-fry

Meg is my middle daughter, a busy doctor and mother of three, and this is one of her fast after-work recipes. Meg uses ready-to-use or 'straight-to-wok' noodles; if you prefer to use dried ones, prepare according to the packet instructions.

Heat the oil in a wok or large saucepan over a medium-high heat, add the onion and cook, stirring, for 3–5 minutes until starting to soften. Add the broccoli along with a splash of cold water, cover the pan and increase the heat to high. Steam the broccoli for 5 minutes, until the stems begin to soften and the water has evaporated. Add the garlic, chilli, ginger, (bell) pepper, mushrooms, sugar snap peas and sweetcorn, and cook for 1–2 minutes until the vegetables are cooked. Stir in the noodles and warm over a low heat until the noodles are heated through. Add soy sauce, to taste.

Serve, garnished with the chopped coriander (cilantro) and roasted cashew nuts.

Serves 2–3

2 tbsp olive oil
1 onion, chopped
125g (4½oz) slim broccoli stalks
3 garlic cloves, grated or crushed
1 red chilli, finely chopped
3cm (1in) piece of fresh root ginger, grated
1 red (bell) pepper, deseeded and thinly sliced
125g (4½oz) button mushrooms
125g (4½oz) sugar snap peas
125g (4½oz) baby sweetcorn, sliced lengthways
300g (10½oz) straight-to-wok noodles
soy sauce, to taste
handful of fresh coriander (cilantro) leaves, chopped, to garnish
roasted cashew nuts, to serve

weekend feasts

Weekends are often the realm of hearty breakfasts, wonderful slices of cake while catching up with friends and family or celebratory meals out. The recipes in this section are perfect for those in-between times when you are looking for something a little lighter, whilst still feeling weekend-worthy. Many of them would also make wonderful starters for a special meal or dinner party.

caesar salad

We love this version of Caesar salad and eat it as a main course in its own right. Of course, classic Caesar salad is generally served as a first course and includes slivers of Parmesan cheese, and you could indeed include vegan Parmesan or perhaps a scattering of the Parmesan on p.263, but we find the combination of lovely crisp Little Gem or Cos lettuce leaves, crunchy croutons warm from the oven and creamy Vegan Mayonnaise (p.258) just perfect as it is.

Serves 2–4

1 long slim or 2 short French sticks (baguettes),
    cut into slices 3mm (⅛in) thick
olive oil, for brushing
1 x recipe quantity Vegan Mayo (p.258)
    (about 150ml/5fl oz/⅔ cup)
a few drops of Tabasco sauce (optional)
1 garlic clove, crushed (optional)
4 Little Gem lettuces, washed and torn into pieces

Preheat the oven to 160°C/325°F/gas mark 3.

Brush the bread slices lightly on both sides with olive oil and place on a baking sheet. Bake for 12–16 minutes, turning once, until golden and crisp on both sides. Check from time to time as some will bake more quickly than others, depending on your oven.

Meanwhile, make the mayonnaise as described on p.258, then flavour it to taste with a little Tabasco sauce and/or crushed garlic, as desired.

To serve, place the lettuce leaves in a bowl, the warm croutons in a basket or separate serving dish and the mayonnaise in another bowl. Let everyone serve themselves and enjoy the delicious flavours and textures.

rainbow salad with carrot and ginger dressing

This pretty salad, with its delicious, easy dressing, was inspired by the one created by Gwyneth Paltrow in her book, *It's All Good*. It makes a stunning first course or light meal – I love it. The dressing keeps well in the refrigerator, so you can make it ahead of time and then put it all together at the last minute.

First, make the dressing. Put all the ingredients except the salt and pepper into a high-powered blender or food processor and process until well combined. Taste, season with salt and pepper and set aside until you are ready to eat.

Arrange the salad ingredients on a shallow serving platter, or individual plates if you prefer, and spoon the dressing between and over some of the vegetables, so that the pretty colours of the salad are on show.

Sprinkle with a few sesame seeds or a little gomasio to serve.

Serves 4

2 little gem lettuces (or similar)
2 tomatoes, halved and thinly sliced
½ cucumber, peeled and sliced
1 small purple onion, sliced
1 tsp sesame seeds or gomasio
(roasted sesame seed and salt
seasoning, see p.268), to garnish

For the carrot and ginger dressing:
150g (5½oz) carrot, sliced
1 small white onion, sliced
thumb-sized piece of fresh root ginger,
peeled
1 tbsp toasted sesame oil
1 tbsp sweet white miso paste
1 tbsp maple syrup
2 tbsp rice vinegar or cider vinegar
2 tbsp water
4 tbsp light olive oil
salt and freshly ground black pepper,
to taste

celeriac terrine with red pepper sauce

Over my years as a cookery writer, I've found it interesting that readers mention certain recipes over and over again – they just seem to go to their hearts. This is one of them, which I invented for my *Vegetarian Four Seasons Cookbook*, published in 1993. I'm including a brand new, veganized version here both for old times' sake and because everyone loves it. I hope you will too! I like it with crunchy, golden roast potatoes that you can cook in the oven at the same time as the terrine. Any leftovers are delicious sliced and served with salad.

Preheat the oven to 200°C/400°F/gas mark 6. Line a 1kg (2lb) loaf tin (pan) with baking paper.

Put the rice into a saucepan with about 175ml (6fl oz/¾ cup water) and bring to the boil, then cover, reduce the heat to very low and cook for 15 minutes.

Meanwhile, boil the celeriac (celery root) in enough water to cover for about 10 minutes, or until tender. Drain well and blot with kitchen paper so that it is completely dry.

Meanwhile, heat the olive oil in a saucepan over a low-medium heat, add the onion and the garlic and fry for about 15 minutes until tender and golden. Stir in the cornflour (cornstarch), then mix in the milk or cream – the mixture will thicken almost immediately. Set aside.

Mash the celeriac thoroughly by hand or preferably in a food processor. Mix in the ground almonds, the onion mixture and the cooked rice. Season to taste.

Sprinkle half of the breadcrumbs over the base of the lined loaf tin and top with the celeriac mixture, smoothing the top. Scatter over the rest of the breadcrumbs, pressing them in lightly, and drizzle with a little olive oil.

Bake for 50 minutes or until the terrine feels firm to the touch, is golden brown and a skewer comes out clean.

Leave the terrine to stand for 5–10 minutes, then run a knife around the sides to loosen and turn it out on to a warmed plate. Garnish with thin slices of red pepper, chopped chives and toasted almonds, and serve with red pepper sauce.

Serves 6–8

100g (3½oz/generous ½ cup) white basmati rice
700g (1lb 9oz) celeriac (celery root) (buying weight), peeled and cut into smallish pieces
2 tbsp olive oil, plus extra for drizzling
1 large onion, chopped
2 large garlic cloves, finely chopped
40g (1½oz/7 tbsp) cornflour (cornstarch)
4 tbsp plant milk or cream
300g (10½oz/3 cups) ground almonds
4 tbsp dried breadcrumbs
salt and freshly ground black pepper, to taste

To serve:

1 x recipe quantity Red Pepper Sauce (p.254), to serve
1 red (bell) pepper, thinly sliced
2 tbsp chopped chives
small handful toasted flaked (slivered) almonds

155

nut croquettes with caper sauce

By popular demand, this is an updated and veganised version of one of my most requested vegetarian recipes: beautiful, crisp nut croquettes – or 'balls' if you like – in a creamy, piquant sauce. They do take a little time to make, but are well worth it and they freeze well.

Serves 4

50g (2oz/¼ cup) Vegan Butter (see p.266) or vegan spread
4 tbsp plain (all-purpose) flour
1 bay leaf
600ml (20fl oz/2½ cups) plant milk of choice
1 tbsp olive oil, plus extra for shallow-frying
1 large onion, finely chopped
100g (3½oz) slightly stale bread
100g (3½oz/generous ¾ cup) cashews
100g (3½oz/ generous ¾ cup) pecans
3 tbsp capers
2 tsp wine vinegar
2 tbsp chopped fresh chives
salt and freshly ground black pepper, to taste

Melt the vegan butter or spread in a saucepan over a low-medium heat. Stir in the flour and cook, stirring, for 1–2 minutes, then add the bay leaf and half of the milk. Bring to a simmer and cook, stirring, for 2–3 minutes until very thick. Remove half of the mixture to a large bowl and set aside. Stir the remaining milk into the pan, beating hard until smooth, then leave the sauce to simmer very gently for a few minutes while you prepare the croquettes.

Meanwhile, heat the oil in a separate pan over a low-medium heat, add the onion and gently fry for 5–10 minutes, until lightly browned.

Put the bread into a food processor with the cashews and pecans and process until finely chopped.

Add the cooked onions to the reserved thick sauce, along with the nutty breadcrumb mixture and some salt and pepper. Mix, adding a little water if necessary, to obtain a firm but soft and pliable consistency. Form the mixture into 20 walnut-sized balls.

Stir the capers, vinegar and chives into the sauce, season with a little salt and pepper and keep warm.

Heat a little olive oil in a frying pan (skillet) over a medium heat and fry the croquettes for 4–5 minutes, turning them as necessary until they are brown and crisp all over. Drain on kitchen paper.

Serve the nut croquettes immediately, in a pool of the caper sauce.

braised vegetables with lemon and parsley

This pretty dish is a favourite in my family. It's versatile and can be served as a starter, side dish, or as the main course itself, in which case some creamy mashed potato or cooked basmati rice go really well with it. If there's any left over, it's good either hot or cold.

Serves 4–6

pared zest and juice of 1 lemon
4 tbsp olive oil
125ml (4fl oz/½ cup) water
bunch of flat-leaf parsley, stalks and
    leaves separated
2 bay leaves
2–3 thyme sprigs
4 large carrots, cut into batons
2 red (bell) peppers, deseeded and
    cut into chunks
225g (8oz) broccoli, cut into florets
225g (8oz) mangetout (snow peas),
    halved lengthways
225g (8oz) button mushrooms
bunch of spring onions (scallions),
    trimmed
salt and freshly ground black pepper,
    to taste

Put the pared lemon zest into a large saucepan along with the olive oil, water, parsley stalks, bay leaves and thyme.

Bring to the boil, then add the carrots and simmer for 5 minutes, then add the (bell) peppers and cook for a further 5 minutes.

Add the broccoli and cook for 4 minutes, then add the mangetout (snow peas), button mushrooms and spring onions (scallions) and cook for a further 2 minutes or so, until all the vegetables are just tender.

Add the lemon juice and season with salt and pepper. Chop the parsley leaves and stir in just before serving.

Weekends are made for family and friends. The recipes on the following pages are those guaranteed crowd-pleasers that are sure to leave smiles on faces, full stomachs and empty plates. There is also a full menu for the ultimate of family meals, the Sunday roast.

sweet potato gratin

This recipe, which I believe originated from the excellent Food for Friends restaurant in Brighton, is a favourite with my family. It is helpful to use a food processor with a slicing blade to cut up the potatoes, but after that the rest is easy. As with the Celeriac Terrine (p.154), we like it served with our favourite red pepper sauce, along with a rocket (arugula) salad, which also offers a contrasting texture.

Serves 4–6

4 large sweet potatoes, thinly sliced
2 large white potatoes, thinly sliced
6–8 garlic cloves, crushed
150ml (5fl oz/⅔ cup) olive oil
3 tbsp finely chopped rosemary
1 tbsp finely chopped thyme
salt and freshly ground black pepper, to taste
1 x recipe quantity Red Pepper Sauce (p.254), to serve
rocket (arugula) leaves, to serve

Preheat the oven to 180°C/350°F/gas mark 4.

Place the sliced potato into a large bowl.

Blend the garlic, olive oil, rosemary and thyme together in a bowl, pour the mixture over the potatoes, season with some salt and pepper and mix well so that all the potato slices are coated and seasoned.

Transfer to a large, shallow ovenproof dish, pressing everything down well and as evenly as possible. Bake for 40–50 minutes, or until you can easily pierce the potatoes with a skewer.

If you have time, let it stand for a few minutes for the juices to settle, then serve with red pepper sauce and some rocket (arugula) leaves.

gratin dauphinoise

This simple yet luxurious dish is a favourite in my home and one we love to eat on special occasions. It's so rich and delicious that it needs little to accompany it, allowing the glorious creamy gratin to speak for itself. If you want to make a special meal of it, it's great served after a fresh leafy green salad as a first course, with a refreshing sorbet, such as raspberry, to finish.

Preheat the grill (broiler) to high.

Put the potato slices into a large wide saucepan along with a 1cm (½in) depth of water, cover, bring to the boil and cook for 7–10 minutes, or until easily pierced with the point of a knife.

Drain off the water, keeping the potatoes in the pan.

Pour half of the olive oil and the vegan cream over the potatoes, and season well with nutmeg, salt and pepper, moving the potato slices gently so that are all well coated.

Use a little of the remaining olive oil to grease a shallow baking dish that will fit under your grill, then pour the potato mixture into the dish, ensuring that the top is more or less level. Pour the remaining olive oil over the top.

Grill (broil) for about 15 minutes or until golden brown and crisp on top and heated through.

note on toppings ...

You could also sprinkle the top with vegan Melting 'Cheese' (see p.262) or vegan 'Parmesan' (see p.263) after cooking.

Serves 4 generously as a main course

1.3kg (2lb 14oz) waxy potatoes, such as Maris Piper, peeled and thinly sliced
2 large garlic cloves, crushed
4 tbsp olive oil
1 × 275ml (9½fl oz) carton vegan single cream
grated nutmeg, to taste
salt and freshly ground black pepper, to taste

easy homemade pizza

Of course you can buy pizzas – even vegan ones – pretty well everywhere these days, but there's something very satisfying about making your own, and it's really easy.

Makes 2 pizzas

For the dough:
150g (5½oz/generous 1 cup) plain (all-purpose) wholemeal flour
150g (5½oz/generous 1 cup) plain (all-purpose) white flour
½ tsp salt
1 × 7g (¼oz) sachet fast-action dried yeast
2 tbsp olive oil
about 200ml (7fl oz/scant 1 cup) warm water

For the sauce and topping:
1 tbsp olive oil
1 onion, chopped
1 × 400g (14oz) can chopped tomatoes
1 tsp dried mixed herbs
½ x recipe quantity Melting 'Cheese' (see p.262) (about 125–175g/ 4½–6oz)
salt and freshly ground black pepper, to taste

To make the dough, put both of the flours into a food processor with the salt, yeast and olive oil and process for 30 seconds. With the motor running, gradually add the warm water through the feed tube of the processor, to make a soft dough. Leave to rise in the processor, with the lid still on, for about 45 minutes until doubled in size.

Preheat the oven to 200°C/400°F/gas mark 6 and put 2 large baking sheets into the oven to heat up.

Meanwhile, make the sauce: heat the olive oil in a saucepan over a low-medium heat, add the onion and fry for 10 minutes until tender. Add the tomatoes and herbs and simmer for a further 10 minutes until thick. Remove from the heat and season with salt and pepper.

Divide the dough in half and roll each piece of dough out as thinly as you can, then place on another large baking sheet. Cover each with tomato sauce and scatter with the 'melting cheese'. Put into the oven on top of the preheated baking sheet – this direct heat will help the pizza crisp up.

Bake for about 15 minutes, until the dough is crisp and the cheese is golden brown.

note on leftover dough ...

There may be more dough base than there is topping to cover it. If so, you can make leftovers into garlic bread. Roll it out thinly, then make some cuts in the top, not quite all the way through. Mix some crushed garlic with olive oil and brush it over the surface of the dough. Bake alongside the pizza.

favourite easy lasagne

Preheat the oven to 200°C/400°F/gas mark 6.

Cook the spinach until wilted. You can steam it, or simply puncture the packet in several places and microwave it for 2–3 minutes. Let it cool until you can handle it, then turn into a colander to drain off any excess liquid.

Meanwhile, put the lasagne sheets into a bowl of freshly boiled water for 1–2 minutes to soften a little.

To assemble the lasagne, put half of the cheese sauce into a baking dish, about 23 × 33cm (9 × 13in), then add a layer of softened lasagne sheets. Top with half of the passata and some basil leaves, then top with another layer of lasagne sheets. Next, layer in the spinach and more lasagne sheets, then top with the rest of the passata and basil and a final layer of lasagne sheets. Top with the remaining cheese sauce and scatter over the crunchy topping.

Bake, uncovered, for 35–40 minutes until puffy and golden brown.

Allow to cool for 20–30 minutes before serving. This helps the layers to firm up and will make it easier to serve.

This may seem like an unusual way to make lasagne, but it works really well and it's delicious. Once you've made the 'cheese' sauce and the crunchy topping, which can both be done in advance, it's very quick to put together. The topping makes more than you'll need for this recipe, but it keeps for 2–3 weeks in the refrigerator and is useful for other recipes where you want a 'cheesy', crunchy finish. You can also vary the layers according to the actual size and shape of your baking dish.

Serves 6–8

1 × 450g (1lb) packet ready-washed spinach leaves
16 vegan pasta sheets
1 x recipe quantity 'Cheese Sauce' (see p.261) (about 600ml/20floz/ 2½ cups)
1 × 400g (14oz) can tomato passata
1 small bunch of fresh basil, leaves torn
3–4 tbsp 'Parmesan' crunchy topping (see p.263)
garlic bread (see p.168), to serve

garlic bread

Preheat the oven to 200°C/400°F/gas mark 6.

Make deep slices along the length of the French stick, about 2cm (¾in) apart, making sure the slices hold together at the base, keeping the stick intact.

Mix together the garlic and the vegan butter or spread, then generously coat both sides of each slice of bread with the garlic butter mixture. Push the loaf back together so that it keeps its shape, then wrap it in foil and place on a baking sheet. Bake for about 20 minutes, or until gorgeously buttery on the inside and crisp on the outside. Serve immediately.

Who doesn't love garlic bread? It makes a hot and welcome accompaniment to many dishes, adding that final welcoming touch – especially when it's homemade, like this, and served hot from the oven. You can also prepare it in advance, wrap in foil and keep in the freezer to bake when you need it. Sizes of French sticks vary – I like a moderately slim one, but any will work.

Serves 2–4

1 French stick
3–4 garlic cloves, crushed
125g (4½oz) soft Homemade Vegan Butter (p.266) or store-bought vegan spread

image p.167

spiced persian pilaf with pomegranate and almonds

This beautiful dish is easy to make, light but satisfying to eat and surprisingly filling. I love to serve it simply, with steamed broccoli spears and perhaps some creamy hummus and fresh dates on the side. To make a feast of it, serve with a Middle Eastern fruit platter for dessert, with some good coffee to finish.

Half-fill a large saucepan (with a lid) with water and bring to the boil. Put the rice into a sieve (strainer), rinse quickly under running cold water, then tip the rice into the saucepan. Bring back to the boil and simmer for 7 minutes. For perfect rice, the timing is important. Drain and shake off excess water, but don't let the rice get too dry.

Rinse and quickly dry the saucepan and put it back on the heat. Add the vegan butter, spices and lemon zest and cook over a gentle heat, stirring, for 1–2 minutes, then stir in the drained rice. Cover with the lid and cook over a very gentle heat for 30 minutes.

Remove from the heat, and gently stir in the spring onions (scallions), almonds, pine nuts and raisins. Season with salt and pepper, then turn the rice out onto a large, warm serving plate, heaping the rice up attractively. Sprinkle with the pomegranate seeds and a nice scattering of fresh parsley and serve.

Serves 4

300g (10½oz/1¾ cups) white basmati rice
generous knob of Vegan Butter (see p.266) or vegan spread
3 cardamom pods, crushed
1 cinnamon stick, broken
a good pinch of saffron (if available)
2 pared strips of lemon zest
2 spring onions (scallions), chopped
50g (2oz/½ cup) blanched almonds, whole or flaked (slivered)
25g (¾oz/scant ¼ cup) toasted pine nuts
50g (2oz/scant ½ cup) raisins or sultanas (golden raisins)
seeds of 1 pomegranate
small handful of flatleaf parsley, leaves roughly chopped
salt and freshly ground black pepper, to taste

image p.170–171

sunday roast menu

SERVES 4

When I was growing up as a vegetarian, in the days before vegetarianism was very well known, the first question I was always asked, by children and adults alike, was 'whatever do you have for Sunday lunch?' Sunday lunch was a much bigger and more conventional event in those days. This is the answer to that question, and I still love it today.

crank's nut roast (p.177)

yorkshire puddings (p.176)

selection of easy vegetable sides (see right)

gravy (p.253)

easy vegetable sides

A dish of vegetables is a lovely, colourful addition to a meal and very quick and easy to prepare. I like to serve at least one accompanying vegetable or salad – or both – with most meals. Here's how:

Wash the vegetables, removing any tough stems or outer leaves, then cut into manageable pieces. Put the pieces into a saucepan with a little boiling water – about 1cm (½in) depth is usually enough – cover and briefly cook until the vegetables feel just tender to the point of a knife, often only about 5 minutes, then drain.

A trick I often use is to par-cook vegetables, take them off the heat but leave them in their cooking water with a lid on the pan, then re-heat them for just 1–2 minutes to make them piping hot for serving, before draining and adding seasonings and any fresh herbs.

Vegetables playing an accompanying role to the main course just need to be nicely cooked; they don't usually require a lot of extra flavouring, although you could add a knob of vegan butter, a spoonful of olive oil, or toasted sesame oil for an Asian flavour. Add salt, freshly ground black pepper or grated nutmeg to taste, and a few chopped fresh herbs, just before serving for colour and extra flavour.

tips for cooking different vegetables

Asparagus: lovely steamed whole; it cooks in just a few minutes – don't let it get soggy!

Aubergine (eggplant): cut into slices or wedges and roast in a little oil at 180°C/375°F/gas mark 5 for 20–30 minutes until tender.

Beans, green: young tender ones are lovely cooked in a little boiling water on top of the stove for a few minutes until just tender.

Beans, broad: if they're very young, slice and cook in boiling water; if older, 'pod' them and cook in boiling water, toss with oil or vegan butter; for perfection, pop the bright green beans out of their grey skins.

Beetroot (beets): cover raw uncooked beetroot with water and simmer gently until it feels tender – this can take 30–40 minutes or more. Drain, cool, then pop the beetroot out of its skin, slice and serve: it's nice sprinkled with a little cider vinegar.

Broccoli heads: trim off the stem – this can actually be peeled, sliced and cooked with the top of the broccoli (I rather like it!). Cut the broccoli into chunky pieces or slices, cook in a little boiling water, as above, until just tender: only a few minutes, don't let it get soggy.

Broccoli spears: trim off any hard ends of the stems, then cook the spears in about 2cm (¾in) boiling water in a covered pan for a few minutes, until tender.

Brussels sprouts: trim and slice, unless they're really tiny and firm and not much bigger than a hazelnut, then quickly cook in about 2cm (¾in) of boiling water until they're only just tender, then drain.

Cabbage, spring: shred and cook as described for Brussels sprouts.

Carrots: scrub or peel as necessary; cook baby ones whole with some of the trimmed stems left in place; slice larger ones into circles or sticks. Cook in boiling water to cover until just tender: 7–15 minutes depending on size. Drain and toss in olive oil or vegan butter if you like; some chopped parsley or dill is nice too.

Cauliflower: trim stem and outer leaves. For 'steaks', make cuts down the centre, right through, about 1cm (½in) apart – you'll only get 2 or 3 out of a cauliflower. Cook as described on p.88. Cut the rest into even-sized pieces and cook in boiling water as described above; or toss in olive oil, place in an even layer in a shallow baking tin (pan) and roast at 200°C/400°F/gas mark 6, for 25–30 minutes or until golden brown and tender.

Courgettes (zucchini): 'top and tail' baby ones and cook in a little boiling water until just tender, as described above; or toss in olive oil and roast as for Cauliflower. Alternatively, mix with sliced aubergine (eggplant), red onions, red and yellow (bell) peppers, 1–2 whole peeled garlic cloves and 2–3 tbsp olive oil to coat; roast at 200°C/400°F/gas mark 6, for 40 minutes until golden brown and tender.

Fennel: I love this aniseedy vegetable! It's crisp and gorgeous sliced into salad; cut into quarters or wedges and cooked in water as described above, or roasted either alone or with other vegetables, see Courgettes (above).

Kale: Remove any tough stem, chop the leaves, then cook in 2–3cm (¾–1in) boiling water in a covered pan for about 7 minutes or until tender. Drain and toss with a little olive oil and seasoning to taste.

Leeks: baby leeks, not much larger than asparagus spears, are delicious just trimmed then cooked whole as described above, drained, and tossed in a little olive oil if you wish – they make a lovely first course, either hot or cold. Larger ones need careful cleaning – slit them down the side and wash between the leaves as necessary, then cut into manageable pieces and cook in water, or toss in oil and roast, see Cauliflower (left).

Mangetout (snow peas): cook very lightly in a little boiling water, or add to a stir-fry. I like to cut them down the centre, making two slimmer pieces – I think they cook better this way and retain their crunch.

Mushrooms: rinse very lightly and pat dry, or wipe with a clean damp cloth; trim the stems, and slice as necessary. Fry in a little olive oil, or roast with other vegetables. White baby mushrooms are also lovely sliced in a salad.

Onions: peel, slice or chop, and fry in olive oil until tender; or cut into rings, quarters or smaller pieces and add to a roast vegetable mix (see above or p.82).

Parsnips: prepare and cook as for Carrots; they're also good mashed or puréed after cooking; they make a lovely addition to a tray of roasted vegetables (see p.81).

Peppers (bell): halve, then remove the central core and seeds. They make a great vessel for a delicious stuffing and are a colourful and tasty addition to a tray of roasted vegetables (p.82).

Potatoes: rinse baby new potatoes and boil in enough water to cover until just tender, 10-15 minutes (don't let them get soggy), then toss in olive oil or vegan butter and serve with some chopped fresh parsley, mint or dill. Older potatoes can be cut into suitably sized pieces and cooked in the same way, then drained and fried in olive oil until golden and crisp or mashed with vegan butter and some plant milk and salt and pepper to taste.

For Roast potatoes: cut peeled potatoes into suitably-sized pieces, par-boil in water for 5–10 minutes until you can pierce them with a knife, then drain; meanwhile, preheat the oven to 200°C/400°F/gas mark 6 and place a roasting tin (pan), with a light swirl of olive oil, into the oven. Add the potatoes to the hot tin, turn them quickly to coat in the oil, and roast for about 45 minutes or until crisp and golden, turning them once or twice during cooking.

For baked potatoes: prick the skins of large potatoes, place on a baking sheet or on the oven shelf and bake at 200–230°C/400–450°F/gas mark 6–8 for about 1 hour, or until crisp on the outside and tender inside when you test with the point of a knife. Or try 'Bircher Potatoes' – a cross between a roast and a baked potato and one of my favourites: halve medium-sized potatoes and place cut-side down on an oiled baking sheet. Bake at 200°C/400°F/gas mark 6 for 30–45 minutes, or until you can easily pierce them with the point of a knife.

Swede (rutabaga): peel thickly, cut into pieces, cover with water, and boil until tender, then mash with vegan butter or olive oil, salt, pepper and grated nutmeg. Or add pieces to a mixture of roasted vegetables (p.81).

Sweetcorn, baby: use whole, or halve larger ones lengthways: hardly needs any cooking and can be added to salads or to a stir-fry for a pretty flash of colour and pleasant texture.

Sweetcorn, on the cob: remove leaves and trim the stem. Cook, covered, in boiling water until tender, about 10 minutes, or rub with oil and cook under the grill (broiler) or over a barbecue until tender and slightly charred. Rub with crushed garlic or other flavourings, such as umeboshi plum, for extra flavour.

Sweet potato: can be prepared in any of the ways described for potatoes, but cooks more quickly. Try it with hummus and some rocket (arugula) for an interesting quick meal.

Tomatoes: for cooking I generally use canned tomatoes, although fresh tomatoes, especially baby tomatoes on the vine, make a colourful and attractive addition to roasted vegetables (p.82).

Turnip: scrub and trim baby turnips (save the green tops to cook separately – see Kale, above) and boil, or roast, until tender.

yorkshire puddings

A traditional British Sunday lunch wouldn't be the same without them! I have tried numerous recipes and finally ended up with this very simple one, which is wonderful, but you must follow the instructions to the letter! You need a 12-hole deep muffin tin (pan), or two 6-hole ones are easier to handle and will remain hotter while you pour in the batter. These are wonderful served with a nut or lentil loaf, roast potatoes, a green vegetable and gravy – or just on their own, with gravy!

Serves 4–6 (makes 12)

8 tbsp vegetable or rapeseed oil
100g (3½oz/¾ cup) plain (all-purpose) flour
250ml (8½fl oz/generous 1 cup) plant milk
   (soy, oat or almond)
½ tsp salt
4 tsp Orgran Egg Replacer Powder
   (see Ingredient Notes on p.15)
8 tbsp cold water

Preheat the oven to 220°C /425°F/gas mark 7.

Pour 2 teaspoons of oil into each of the holes in the muffin tin's (pan's) and place in the oven to heat up while you make the batter.

In a large jug, whisk together the flour, milk and salt until smooth and set aside.

Once the oven has reached its full heat and the oil is smoking hot, finish making the batter. Whisk the egg-replacer powder

and the water together until the mixture is like fluffy whisked egg (don't try to do this in advance; you must do it just before you put it into the batter). Get it as voluminous as you can, so that it holds its shape. Give the flour mixture in the jug another quick whisk, then gently fold the 'egg' mixture into it with a metal spoon.

Carefully remove the hot tin's from the oven and equally pour the mixture into each hole as quickly as you can. Bake on the top shelf of the oven for about 15–20 minutes, until the Yorkshire puddings are risen and starting to crisp at the edges, but are still light in colour.

Remove the tins from the oven and make a hole in the top of each pudding: push the handle of a teaspoon into each pudding to 'pop' it, twist well and push back the sides to make a hollow in the middle. Return the tins to the oven and bake for a further 15 minutes or so, until the puddings are golden brown and cooked through.

crank's nut roast

I knew Kay and David Canter back when they were opening the first of their Cranks' restaurants at the same time that my first books, *Simply Delicious* and *Not Just a Load of Old Lentils*, were being published. We shared excitement and joy about the way that vegetarian food was beginning to 'take off'. I'm including this popular, classic recipe for their nut roast in tribute to them, and also because it's very easy to make, naturally vegan and absolutely delicious. If there's any left over, it's also good cold.

Preheat the oven to 180°C/350°F/gas mark 4. Grease a shallow casserole dish, 20-cm (8-in) cake tin (pan) or a large loaf tin (pan).

Heat the olive oil in a frying pan (skillet) over a low-medium heat, add the onion and fry for 10 minutes, until translucent.

Meanwhile, put the nuts and bread into a food processor and process until fine.

Dissolve the Marmite (yeast extract) in the hot vegetable stock and add to the breadcrumb mixture along with the mixed herbs to form a soft mixture. Season with salt and pepper to taste.

Tip the nut mixture into the prepared dish or tin and bake for 30 minutes until golden brown.

Let stand for 5 minutes before slicing.

Serves 4

2 tbsp olive oil, plus extra for greasing
1 medium onion, finely chopped
225g (8oz/scant 2 cups) mixed nuts (cashews, hazelnuts, almonds, peanuts, walnuts)
100g (3½oz) soft wholemeal bread, crusts removed
2 tsp Marmite (yeast extract)
300ml (10fl oz/1¼ cups) hot vegetable stock (bouillon)
2 tsp mixed dried herbs
salt and freshly ground black pepper, to taste

Whether planning a celebration meal with friends or a romantic supper for two, we all have those occasions where we want to put something that extra bit special on the table. The recipes on the following pages are my go-tos for those days. I love them and hope that you do, too.

cauliflower steaks with saffron mayo

Cauliflower 'steaks' are one of my favourite dishes and so easy to make. You do need a firm, not too large cauliflower, and you will only get about two, or at the most three, steaks out of it, because the florets around it will become detached from the core. Here, the steaks are roasted and served with a topping of saffron mayonnaise, but they can also be topped with other delicious things: try slices of roasted pepper or a splash of Red Pepper Sauce (p.254); some Pesto (p.96); or fried wild or button mushrooms.

Serves 2–3

1 medium firm cauliflower
olive oil, for brushing
toasted pine nuts, to garnish

For the saffron mayonnaise:
1 x recipe quantity of Vegan Mayo (p.258)
a good pinch of saffron strands

Preheat the oven to 200°C/400°F/gas mark 6. Trim the cauliflower and cut down from the top to make 2 or 3 thick slices ('steaks') that hold together. Put them onto a baking sheet and brush on both sides with oil. Bake for about 20 minutes, until tender to the point of a knife and lightly browned.

Meanwhile, make the mayonnaise as described on p.258. Soak a few saffron strands in a teaspoon of hot water for 1–2 minutes, then stir the mixture into the mayonnaise.

Serve the baked cauliflower steaks topped with a generous spoonful of the mayonnaise and a scattering of toasted pine nuts.

chestnut-stuffed mushrooms on potato rostis

Preheat the oven to 180°C/350°F/gas mark 4.

Season the grated potato, then divide the mixture into 4 equal quantities.

Heat a little olive oil in one or two large frying pans (skillets) over a low-medium heat, place each portion of potato into the pan/s and press down on each with a fish slice or spatula to flatten into large cakes, slightly larger than the mushrooms. Fry until the first sides are golden brown, 9–10 minutes, then flip them over and fry the other sides likewise. Transfer to a baking sheet.

In the same pan, fry the mushrooms in a little more olive oil on both sides for 2–3 minutes, until they start to become tender. Place each mushroom, gill-side up, on each of the rostis.

Next, make the stuffing. Heat the olive oil in a saucepan over a low-medium heat, add the onion and fry for about 10 minutes until tender, then stir through the chestnuts, lemon juice and shoyu or tamari sauce. Mash the mixture roughly, with a fork or in a food processor, until coarsely chopped and holding together. Season, to taste.

Divide the chestnut mixture between the mushrooms, heaping it up. Bake in the oven for about 15 minutes.

Serve immediately, scattered with a little chopped parsley.

For me, these say 'Christmas on a plate'. They're easy to make, beautiful to look at and delicious to eat, and particularly satisfying when you can forage in the countryside for some of the ingredients (the mushrooms and chestnuts – although they can also be easily found in the shops). The dish can be prepared in advance as far as the final heating, making it ideal for relaxed entertaining. Serve accompanied by a cooked leafy vegetable (see p.173–5), a quick gravy and some cranberry sauce.

Serves 4

800g (1lb 12oz) baking potatoes, peeled and coarsely grated
4 field or Portobello mushrooms (about 10cm/4in wide), trimmed and wiped clean
olive oil, for frying
salt and freshly ground black pepper, to taste
fresh parsley, chopped, to garnish

For the stuffing:
2 tbsp olive oil
1 red onion, sliced
1 × 200g (7oz) packet whole natural chestnuts (peeled, cooked and ready to use), roughly chopped
2 tbsp fresh lemon juice
1 tbsp shoyu or tamari sauce
salt and freshly ground black pepper, to taste

marinated tofu with asparagus, and sea vegetables

This is very quick to put together – it's something I came up with one evening for supper when there was nothing much in the fridge but I wanted to use up some asparagus, button mushrooms and tofu! The sea vegetable garnish is optional, but makes a nice flourish on top. I love sea veg and keep several different types in my store cupboard, see p.12–15.

This makes enough for two people but the quantities can easily be doubled for four.

In a shallow bowl, mix together the marinade ingredients. Carefully unwrap the tofu and gently cut into slices about 6mm (¼in) thick. Place the slices into the marinade and leave to marinate for at least 15 minutes.

Meanwhile, put the rice into a saucepan with the water and bring to the boil, then cover, reduce the heat to very low and cook for 15 minutes. About 5 minutes before the end of cooking, remove the lid, set a sieve (strainer) with the asparagus in it over the pan, and replace the lid or cover with a plate to keep in the steam.

Once cooked, stir the rice with a fork, then set the pan aside, still covered.

Heat a little olive oil in a frying pan (skillet) over a medium heat and fry the mushrooms for 1–2 minutes. Remove and keep warm.

Heat a little toasted sesame oil in a frying pan over a medium heat, place the tofu slices in the pan and fry until browned on one side, 5–6 minutes, then turn the pieces over and cook the other side likewise.

To serve, place a heap of rice in the middle of each plate, arrange the fried tofu slices, mushrooms and asparagus on top, stacking them attractively. Drizzle over a little shoyu and top with some snipped nori or soaked sea vegetables.

Serves 2

1 × 225g (8oz) packet firm tofu
90g (3oz/½ cup) white basmati rice
175ml (6fl oz/¾ cup) water
125g (4½oz) trimmed asparagus spears
    (trimmed weight)
200g (7oz) baby white mushrooms,
    sliced
toasted sesame oil and olive oil,
    for frying
shoyu soy sauce, for drizzling
snipped nori sheets or soaked
    Japanese sea vegetables
    (see p.15), to serve

For the marinade:
1 garlic clove, finely crushed
3 tbsp shoyu

chilli polenta cakes with mushrooms and spinach

This has a bit of the 'wow' factor about it, and everyone loves it: crisp polenta 'cakes' with chilli jam, stacked up on tender spinach leaves, served with tender fried red onions, wild mushrooms and asparagus. It's a lovely way to celebrate the first of the summer's asparagus. I use store-bought chilli relish and instant polenta, which both taste great and save a lot of time. In fact, I often make up the whole packet of polenta, as the polenta cakes freeze very well either before or after cooking.

To make the polenta cakes, bring the water and salt to the boil in a saucepan. While stirring with a whisk, sprinkle in the polenta until you have a smooth mixture, then reduce the heat to a simmer and cook for 8 minutes.

Turn the still-hot polenta onto a board and press it out to about 1½cm (½in) thick. Stamp out 12 rounds with a 7 cm (2¾ in) pastry cutter, re-rolling the off-cuts at the end.

Add the soya milk and flour to a shallow bowl, then mix to a paste. Place the panko breadcrumbs in a separate bowl. Dip each piece of polenta first into the soya milk mixture, then into the breadcrumbs to coat both sides.

Heat a little olive oil in a frying pan (skillet) over a medium heat until very hot. Fry the polenta cakes until golden brown all over, a good 3–4 minutes on each side. Transfer to a baking sheet or plate and keep warm in a low oven.

Fry the onions in the same pan in a little olive oil until they are beautifully soft and sweet. Set aside and keep warm. Then do the same with the mushrooms.

Place the spinach in a saucepan, add 1–2 tablespoons of water, cover and cook over a medium heat until collapsed and tender, about 2 minutes, then drain.

Cook the asparagus in 2cm (¾in) of boiling water in a saucepan for about 7 minutes or so, until just tender.

To serve, put some of the cooked spinach leaves, a little heap of the onions, some asparagus spears and mushrooms onto each plate. Place 2 crisp polenta cakes on top of each serving, drizzling or spreading t hem generously with chilli relish.

Serves 4–6

750 ml (26fl oz/3¼ cups) water

½ tsp salt

½ × 375g (13oz) packet instant polenta (cornmeal)

5 tbsp soya milk

45g (1⅔oz/⅓ cup) plain (all-purpose) flour

75g (2⅔oz/1½ cups) panko breadcrumbs, crushed

olive oil, for frying

2 large red onions, halved and thinly sliced

500g (1lb 2oz) mixed wild mushrooms, sliced

400g (14oz) fresh baby spinach leaves

450g (1lb) tender asparagus, trimmed

1 × 320g (11½oz) jar hot habañero chilli relish (you won't need it all)

image p.186-187

185

weekend feasts

vegan wellington

Preheat the oven to 200°C/400°F/gas mark 6.

Heat 1 tablespoon of the oil in a saucepan over a low-medium heat, add the onion and fry for 10 minutes, then add the mushrooms and garlic and cook, stirring, for a further 5 minutes. Remove from the heat.

Put the cashews and bread into a food processor and process to fine crumbs, then add the onion and mushroom mixture, tarragon, shoyu, yeast extract and lemon juice and process until smooth. Season with salt and pepper to taste.

Spread the puff pastry sheet out on the work surface, with the shorter edges at the sides. Place the nut mixture in a rectangle down the centre of the pastry (about 8cm/3in wide), leaving 2cm (¾in) clear at the top and bottom edges. With a sharp knife, make diagonal cuts in the side pieces of pastry, starting from the top left corner and working towards the filling at about a 45-degree angle, making each strip about 1cm (½in) wide. Repeat on the other side, starting at the top right corner, cutting down towards the filling. Enclose the filling with the pastry strips: fold the end pieces in first, then alternately fold over diagonal strips from each side to create a plaited effect – this is much easier than it sounds. Brush the pastry with soya milk.

Gently transfer the pastry to a baking sheet and bake for 45–60 minutes, until it is puffed up, crisp and golden.

If you're looking for a centrepiece main course for a special dinner, I don't think you can beat this: a tasty nut pâté mixture encased in crisp, golden puff pastry. It looks and tastes wonderful, is easy to make and can be prepared in advance. Serve it in winter with vegan gravy, cranberry sauce, Brussels sprouts and roast potatoes, or in summer with braised seasonal vegetables.

Serves 6

2 tbsp olive oil
1 onion, chopped
200g (7oz) button mushrooms, sliced
1 garlic clove, crushed
200g (7oz/1¾ cups) cashews
100g (3½oz) fresh white bread
1 tsp dried tarragon
2 tbsp shoyu soy sauce
1 tsp Marmite (yeast extract)
1 tbsp freshly squeezed lemon juice
250g (9oz) ready-rolled puff pastry
soya milk, for brushing
salt and freshly ground black pepper, to taste

celebration white nut roast with herb stuffing

Here is the answer to the question people always ask vegetarians and vegans: 'what on earth do you eat for Christmas dinner?', and as far as I'm concerned, it's a really delicious nut roast – in particular, this beautiful white one with parsley stuffing. My daughter loves it so much that she chose it for the main course at her wedding reception, and it tasted just as good eaten in a marquee in a beautiful garden on a perfect midsummer's evening, as the sun set and the stars began to shine.

Preheat the oven to 180°C/350°F/gas mark 4. Grease and line a 900g (2lb) loaf tin (pan) with baking paper.

To make the white nut mixture, melt the butter and oil in a large saucepan over a low-medium heat and cook the onions for 10–15 minutes until they are soft and tender. Remove from the heat, then stir in all the other ingredients. Season with salt and pepper and set aside.

To make the green stuffing mixture, simply blend all the ingredients together in a food processor, then season.

To assemble, put half of the white mixture into the tin, then top with the green stuffing mixture, ensuring the white layer is covered. Spread the rest of the white mixture on top and press down lightly. Dot the surface of the loaf with vegan butter and top with baking paper.

Bake for 45 minutes, then remove the paper and bake for a further 15 minutes, until golden brown.

Serves 6

Vegan Butter (p.266) or vegan spread, for greasing and topping
salt and freshly ground black pepper, to taste

For the white nut mixture:
40g (1½oz/3 tbsp) Vegan Butter (p.266) or vegan spread
1½ tbsp olive oil
2 onions, finely chopped
300g (10½oz/2½ cups) cashews, finely ground
175g (6oz/3 cups) soft white breadcrumbs
8–10 tbsp water or vegetable stock (bouillon)
grated nutmeg, to taste

For the green stuffing mixture:
175g (6oz/3 cups) soft white breadcrumbs
grated zest and juice of 1 lemon
2 tsp dried Herbes de Provence
6 tbsp chopped flat-leaf parsley
50g (2oz/3½ tbsp) Vegan Butter (p.266) or vegan spread

vegetable and melting 'cheese' quiche

This is a delicious, deep, traditional quiche.

Serves 4–6

For the easy pastry:
300g (10½oz/2¼ cups) plain (all-purpose) flour
1 pinch salt
200g (7oz/generous ¾ cup) Vegan Butter (see p.266) or vegan spread
4–6 tbsp cold water

For the filling:
2 onions (red or white), sliced
1 red (bell) pepper, deseeded and cut into roughly 2-cm (¾-in) pieces
100g (3½oz) thin asparagus spears, trimmed
2 tbsp olive oil
1 x recipe quantity 'Melting Cheese' (see p.262), made up to the point just before chilling
salt and freshly ground black pepper, to taste

Preheat the oven to 200°C/400°F/gas mark 6.

Spread the vegetables for the filling over a baking sheet in a single layer, drizzle with the olive oil and roast for about 25 minutes until tender.

Meanwhile, make the pastry. Combine the flour, salt and vegan butter in a bowl and rub in the fat to the consistency of breadcrumbs. Alternatively, process the ingredients together in a food processor until just combined (some flecks of butter can remain). Gradually add the cold water until the mixture comes together; the less water you use, the crisper the pastry will be.

Form the pastry into a ball, flatten it slightly and place it between 2 sheets of greaseproof paper. Thinly roll out the pastry to fit a deep 25-cm (10-in) diameter quiche tin (tart pan). Peel off the top layer of paper and use the bottom layer to transfer the pastry to the tin. Peel off the remaining paper, press the pastry into the tin and trim the edges. Prick the base, then bake for 10 minutes, until firm and just golden brown. Remove from the oven and set aside.

Reduce the oven temperature to 180°C/350°F/gas mark 4.

To assemble the quiche, spread the roasted vegetables over the pastry case in an even layer, then spoon over the 'melting cheese' mixture, letting some of the colourful vegetables show through. Bake for about 30 minutes, until the filling is set and lightly browned in places. Remove from the oven and let stand for a few minutes, then remove from the tin to a warm serving plate. It's delicious hot, but lovely cold too.

red onion and melting 'cheese' tart

Preheat the oven to 200°C/400°F/gas mark 6.

Make the pastry in the same way described in the recipe for Roasted Vegetable and Melting Cheese Quiche (left), then form the pastry into a ball, flatten it slightly and place it between 2 large sheets of greaseproof paper. Thinly roll out the pastry to fit a 20-cm (8-in) shallow flan tin (tart pan). Peel off the top layer of paper and use the bottom layer of paper to transfer the pastry to the tin. Peel off the paper, press the pastry into the tin and trim the edges. Prick the base all over, then bake for 10 minutes, until firm and just golden brown. Remove from the oven and set aside.

Meanwhile, make the filling. Heat the oil in a large saucepan with a lid over a medium heat, add the onions, stir to coat in the oil, then cover and cook for about 15 minutes, until very soft and tender, stirring every 5 minutes. Remove the lid, add the sugar, sherry and vinegar and cook gently, uncovered, for about 15 minutes, until there is hardly any liquid left. Season with salt and pepper and leave to cool.

Reduce the oven temperature to 180°C/350°F/gas mark 4.

To assemble the tart, spread the red onion mixture over the pastry case in an even layer. Arrange the circles of 'melting cheese' on top, leaving some gaps for the red onion mixture to show through. Bake for about 20 minutes, until the 'cheese' is bubbling and golden brown in places.

Remove from the oven and let stand for a few minutes, then remove from the tin to a warm serving plate.

This is a vegan version of one of my family's all-time favourite dishes. I hope you will enjoy it as much as we do. You do need to make the 'melting cheese' for the topping in advance (see p.262), but as long as you allow time for that, it's easy. The pastry case and the red onion filling can both be made in advance too, and the tart can then be quickly assembled just before cooking. It's delicious served with a mixed baby leaf salad and perhaps some new potatoes or creamy mash alongside.

Serves 4–6

For the easy pastry:
225g (8oz/1¾ cups) plain (all-purpose) flour
1 pinch salt
150g (5oz/⅔ cup) Vegan Butter (see p.266) or vegan spread
up to 6 tbsp cold water

For the filling:
2 tbsp olive oil
1kg (2lb 3oz) red onions, thinly sliced
2 tbsp sugar
3 tbsp sherry or sweet white wine
2 tbsp red wine vinegar
1 x recipe quantity 'Melting Cheese' (see p.262), sliced into thin circles
salt and freshly ground black pepper, to taste

image p.194-195

weekend feasts

193

aubergine pilaf cake

This makes a stunning centrepiece for a feast – it really does have the 'wow' factor and needs little in the way of accompaniments: a few feathery rocket (arugula) leaves and some thick, garlicky thick vegan yogurt. It does take a while to make, but you can do all the preparation and cooking in advance, then just sit back and enjoy the feast with everyone else!

Preheat the oven to 180°C/350°F/gas mark 4.

Spread the pine nuts out on a baking sheet and toast in the oven for 1–2 minutes until just golden. Remove from the heat as soon as they're *just* done. Set aside.

Heat a little olive oil in a frying pan (skillet) over a medium heat, add the aubergine (eggplant) slices in batches and fry for 3–4 minutes on each side until tender and golden brown. Remove to drain on kitchen paper.

Meanwhile, cook the rice. Half-fill a large saucepan with water and bring to the boil. Put the rice into a sieve (strainer), rinse quickly under running cold water, then tip the rice into the saucepan. Bring back to the boil and simmer for 7 minutes, then drain.

Put the rice in a bowl and mix with two-thirds of the toasted pine nuts, the raisins, vegan butter, ground cinnamon and chilli flakes. Season with salt and set aside.

Steam the washed spinach in a dry saucepan over a medium heat for 2–3 minutes, until wilted. Drain off any excess water in a colander and squeeze the spinach to ensure it is fairly dry.

To assemble, closely arrange the aubergine slices to line the sides and base of the cake tin, without leaving any gaps. Spread half of the spinach in the bottom of the tin, then put in all of the rice mixture, pressing it down firmly. Put the remaining spinach on top of the rice and press down. If there are any spare aubergine slices, place them on top – this will be the base of the pilaf when turned out.

Bake for 20 minutes. Remove from the oven and let stand for 5–10 minutes before turning out onto a large plate. Scatter over the remaining toasted pine nuts and some fresh coriander (cilantro), to garnish. Slice and serve.

Serves 6

100g (3½oz/¾ cup) pine nuts

olive oil, for frying

3–4 medium aubergines (eggplant), trimmed and cut into 1-cm (½-in) thick slices

300g (10½oz/1¾ cups) white basmati rice

100g (3½oz/¾ cup) raisins

40g (1½oz/3 tbsp) Vegan Butter (see p.266) or vegan spread

2 tsp ground cinnamon

½ tsp dried chilli flakes

450g (1lb) tender spinach leaves, washed

salt and freshly ground black pepper, to taste

small bunch of fresh coriander (cilantro), torn, to garnish

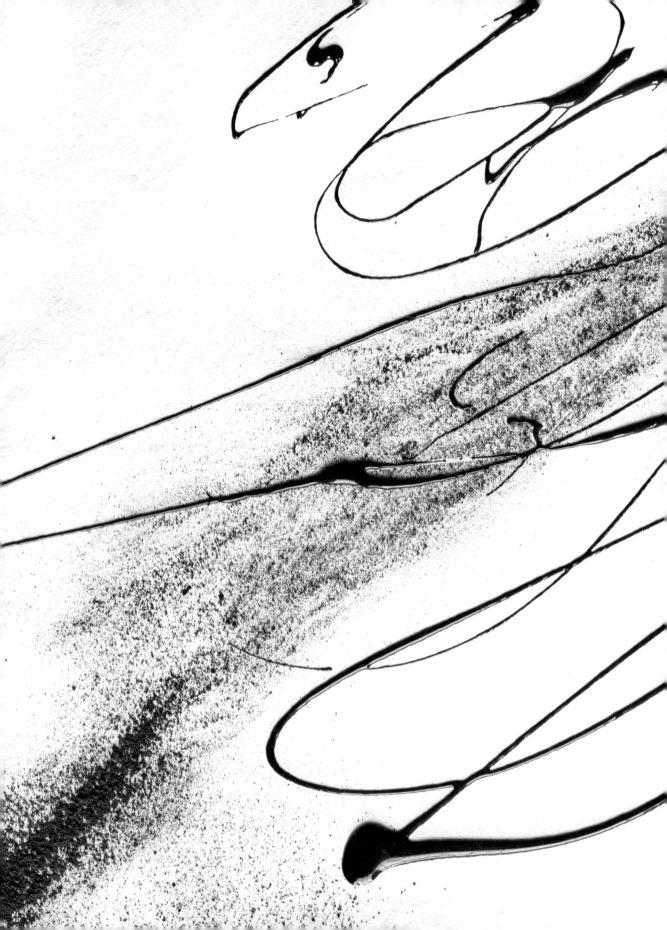

desserts

microwave chocolate sponge pudding

A lovely, quick treat for one that you can rustle up in a few minutes in a cup or a mug. Thanks to my daughter Meg for this recipe, which has often been enjoyed by my twin teenage grandsons.

Serves 1

½ tsp cider vinegar

50ml (2fl oz/3½ tbsp) soya milk

50g (2oz/¼ cup) caster (superfine) sugar

25g (1oz/scant 2 tbsp) Vegan Butter (see p.266) or vegan spread, plus extra for greasing

50g (2oz/generous ⅓ cup) self-raising (self-rising) flour

2 tbsp unsweetened cocoa powder

a pinch of baking powder

½ tsp vanilla extract

2 tbsp golden syrup

Combine the cider vinegar and soya milk in a bowl and set aside to curdle.

In a separate bowl, mix the sugar and vegan butter or spread until well combined. Add the flour, cocoa, baking powder and vanilla extract and mix thoroughly. Pour in the curdled milk and mix until well combined.

Grease the inside of a microwaveable cup or mug with vegan butter or spread, then spoon in the golden syrup to make a layer at the bottom. Spoon the pudding batter into the cup on top of the syrup.

Microwave on full power for 1½ minutes or until risen and firm to a light touch. Turn out into a bowl and enjoy.

blueberry crumble

This is a very easy, delicious pudding. It also works perfectly using gluten-free flour.

Serves 3–4

400g (14oz/3 cups) blueberries
3 tbsp maple syrup

For the topping:
200g (7oz/1½ cups) self-raising flour
30g (1oz/4 tbsp) walnut halves
a pinch of salt
5 tbsp light olive oil or rapeseed (canola) oil
4 tbsp maple syrup
1 tbsp demerara (turbinado) sugar

Preheat the oven to 180°C/350°F/gas mark 4.

Put the blueberries into an ovenproof dish, about 20cm (8in) square and 5cm (2in) deep. Mix in the maple syrup.

For the topping, put all the ingredients into a food processor and pulse briefly a few times to mix to a lumpy crumble mixture. Spoon the topping lightly over the top of the blueberries.

Bake for 20–25 minutes until the topping is crisp and golden brown and the blueberries are cooked and juicy.

crêpes suzette

First, make the crêpes. Combine the flour, baking powder and salt in a bowl, then whisk in the milk and olive oil to make a smooth batter.

Heat 1–2 tablespoons olive oil in a frying pan (skillet) over a medium heat. Once hot, pour off any excess oil onto a saucer. Quickly stir the vinegar into the batter mixture, then pour or ladle a little batter into the hot pan, tipping the pan as necessary to spread the batter to cover the surface of the pan.

Cook for about 30 seconds, or until the crêpe has set and you can lift the edges. Flip the crêpe over and fry the other side for a few seconds. Remove from the pan to a plate and set aside.

Fry the remaining batter in the same way. The mixture should make about 6 pancakes.

Put all the sauce ingredients except the brandy into a large frying pan, or shallow flameproof dish, and heat gently to melt the butter and sugar.

Turn off the heat, then dip the crêpes into the sauce, one by one, coating each side, then folding it in half and half again to make a triangular shape. As each crêpe is done, push it to the side of the pan. When all the crêpes have been dipped, leave in the frying pan or dish until ready to serve.

When ready to serve, set the pan or dish over the heat to warm. As soon as the crêpes are heated right through, increase the heat to high for about 1 minute to make the sauce very hot. Quickly pour in the brandy and set it alight. You can take it to the table at this point, while it is still flaming – the flames will die down in a few seconds, as soon as all the alcohol has burned off. Serve immediately.

This is a lovely vegan version of this French classic. It's a great dish for entertaining because, although it may seem like quite a lot of work, it's actually quite easy. The crêpes and refreshing orange sauce can be made in advance, then heated through in the pan at the last minute, finishing with the brandy flaming, if you like. Quite dramatic and utterly delicious.

Serves 4–6

mild olive oil, for frying

For the batter:
100g (3½oz/¾ cup) plain (all-purpose) flour
1 tsp baking powder
¼ tsp salt
200ml (7fl oz/scant 1 cup) plant-based milk
2 tbsp mild olive oil
1 tsp cider vinegar or wine vinegar (red or white)

For the sauce:
125g (4½oz/generous ½ cup) Vegan Butter (see p.266) or vegan spread
150g (5oz/¾ cup) caster (superfine) sugar
zest and juice of 3 small-medium oranges
zest and juice of 1 lemon
2 tbsp orange liqueur, such as curaçao (optional)
4 tbsp brandy

lemon cheesecake

I first invented this lemon cheesecake for some non-vegans – they weren't even vegetarians, come to that, but they just couldn't believe that it contained no dairy. They have been making it ever since! I hope you will enjoy the recipe just as much.

Mix the crushed biscuits (crackers) with the melted vegan butter or spread. Pack the mixture into a 20cm (8in) round, loose-bottomed cake tin (pan) and press down well. Set aside in a cool place, ideally the refrigerator, while you make the topping.

Drain the liquid from the cans of coconut milk and discard. Put the solidified coconut cream into a food processor, along with the ground almonds, sugar, coconut oil, vanilla extract and lemon zest and juice. Process gently to combine all the ingredients.

Spoon the topping mixture onto the biscuit base and smooth the top. Chill thoroughly until set, about 2 hours. Decorate with some thin pared curls of lemon zest.

Serves 6–8

For the base:
200g (7oz/1½ cups) vegan digestive biscuits (graham crackers), crushed
100g (3½oz/scant ½ cup) Vegan Butter (see p.266) or vegan spread, melted

For the filling:
2 × 400g (14oz) cans full-fat coconut milk, refrigerated
300g (10½oz/3 cups) ground almonds
60g (2oz/5 tbsp) caster (superfine) sugar
60ml (2fl oz/¼ cup) melted coconut oil
1 tsp vanilla extract
zest and juice of 1 lemon, plus extra pared curls of lemon zest, to serve

frangipane tart

This is one of my favourite dessert recipes: light, crisp pastry with a frangipane topping over a delicate layer of jam. Everyone who tries it loves it, so I hope you will too.

Mix all the ingredients for the pastry together in a bowl by hand, until the mixture forms a dough. Alternatively, blitz in a food processor for 1 minute until well combined.

Form the pastry into a ball, flatten it slightly and place it between 2 large sheets of greaseproof paper. Thinly roll out the pastry to fit a 25cm (10in) round shallow flan tin (tart pan). Prick the pastry all over with a fork, then place in the freezer for 20 minutes.

Meanwhile, preheat the oven to 180°C/350°F/gas mark 4.

Bake the tart case for 18–20 minutes until just golden at the edges, then set aside to cool.

Meanwhile, place all the filling ingredients into a food processor and mix to a smooth batter.

Cover the bottom of the cooled tart case with enough jam (jelly) to form a thin layer (the quantity can be adjusted to taste; the more jam, the sweeter the tart), then pour over the frangipane batter mixture to cover.

Bake for a further 30 minutes until the filling is puffed up and golden. Set aside to cool.

To decorate, add about 2½–3 tsp water to the icing (confectioners') sugar to make a thin glacé frosting. Cover the tart with a thin layer of the frosting, then pipe over the melted chocolate to finish.

Serves 6–8

For the pastry:
225g (8oz/1¾ cups) plain (all-purpose) flour
25g (1oz/¼ cup) ground almonds
150g (5oz/⅔ cup) pure coconut oil or Vegan Butter (see p.266) or vegan spread
a pinch of salt

For the frangipane filling:
180g (6oz/1¾ cups) ground almonds
90g (3oz/scant ½ cup) caster (superfine) sugar
75g (2½oz/⅓ cup) vegan spread
2 tbsp cornflour (cornstarch)
180ml (6fl oz/¾ cup) almond milk
1 tsp vanilla extract
1½ tsp almond extract
a pinch of salt

To decorate:
about 200g (7oz) raspberry jam (jelly) (about ½ jar)
80g (3oz/½ cup) icing (confectioners') sugar
50g (2oz) dark (bittersweet) chocolate, melted

eton mess

Serves 4

500g (1lb 2oz) fresh raspberries
½ x recipe quantity of Vegan
   Meringues (p.244)
1 x recipe quantity of Vegan Double
   Cream (p.267)

This is probably my favourite dessert, so I was thrilled when I discovered how easy it is to make vegan meringues and double cream: it really is heavenly. You can make a wonderful version of it using Vegan Meringues (p.244), Vegan Double Cream (p.267) and raspberries.

Although you will only need about half of the meringues for this recipe, it's easiest to make the full batch, because it uses exactly the amount of liquid one usually gets from a can of chickpeas (garbanzo beans) and any less would be tiresome to whisk. You could use the remaining half sandwiched with cream or in any other way you fancy – they will keep for a day or two, but they quickly disappear, I promise you!

Divide the raspberries among 4 serving bowls. Crumble 3–4 meringues into each bowl, then add 3 large spoonfuls of the double cream to each. Gently mix together to make a lovely melange and serve immediately.

lovely fruit salad

Holding the oranges over a bowl to catch the juice, use a sharp, serrated knife to cut off the peel and white pith, going round and round with a sawing motion. Cut the orange segments away from the white inner pith and add to the bowl.

Halve the melon, scoop out and discard the seeds, then scoop the flesh away from the skin using a melon-baller or knife and add to the bowl.

Finally, add the strawberries, grapes, kiwi fruit and orange juice and gently mix to combine, adding a little maple syrup for extra sweetness, if you like.

Such a simple dessert, but one that really does have the 'wow' factor when it's well made with a variety of pretty fruits and served with Golden Crunch Biscuits (see p.226) and a generous amount of coconut cream (p.244).

Serves 4

2 oranges
1 small melon (pale green or orange flesh – you choose)
175g (6oz) strawberries, hulled
225g (8oz) black grapes, halved and deseeded
2 kiwi fruit, peeled and sliced
150ml (5fl oz/⅔ cup) orange juice
a little maple syrup, to sweeten (optional)

treacle tart

This is a long-standing favourite in my family – very easy to make and loved by all.

Preheat the oven to 200°C/400°F/gas mark 6.

To make the pastry, combine the flour, salt and vegan butter in a bowl and rub in the fat to the consistency of breadcrumbs. Alternatively, process the ingredients together in a food processor until just combined (some flecks of butter can remain). Gradually add the cold water until the mixture comes together; the less water you use, the crisper the pastry will be.

Form the pastry into a ball, flatten it slightly and place it between 2 large sheets of greaseproof paper. Thinly roll out the pastry to fit a 20-cm (8-in) diameter shallow flan tin (tart pan). Peel off the top layer of paper and use the bottom layer of paper to transfer the pastry to the tin. Peel off the paper, press the pastry into the tin and trim the edges. Prick the base all over, then bake for 10 minutes, until firm and just golden brown. Remove from the oven and set aside.

Reduce the oven temperature to 180°C/350°F/gas mark 4.

For the filling, put the syrup into a large saucepan and warm gently until liquid. Stir in the breadcrumbs and leave to cool slightly.

Pour the syrup mixture into the pastry case and bake for 20–25 minutes until the pastry is crisp and the filling is golden brown and set but not dry. Serve while still warm.

Serves 4–6

For the easy pastry:
225g (8oz/1¾ cups) plain (all-purpose) flour
1 pinch salt
150g (5oz/⅔ cup) Vegan Butter (see p.266) or vegan spread
up to 6 tbsp cold water

For the filling:
450g (1lb/scant 1½ cups) golden syrup
125g (4½oz/2 cups) soft fresh breadcrumbs

claire's ice cream

Serves 8

700ml (1¼ pints/scant 3 cups)
  soya milk
1 × 400ml (14fl oz) can full-fat coconut
  milk
250g (9oz/1 cup) caster (superfine)
  sugar
150g (5½oz) barley malt extract
80g (2¾oz/generous ¼ cup)
  coconut oil
100g (3½oz) 85% dark chocolate
½ tsp guar or xanthan gum

Like her sisters, my youngest daughter, Claire, is a keen vegan. When I first tasted this ice cream that she makes, I couldn't believe it was vegan! Claire likes to add the malt extract and chocolate to remind her of her favourite chocolates from her pre-vegan days, but at that stage you could substitute other flavours, for example fresh or frozen fruit, ginger – the possibilities are endless. If you have an ice cream maker the result will be effortlessly smooth and creamy, but can be made just as easily with a freezer. Adding the guar or xanthan gum makes it easier to scoop from the freezer, but does affect the texture; if you choose to omit this, just allow a little time to soften the ice cream before serving.

Combine the soya and the coconut milk in a large pan over a low heat. Once warmed, add the sugar, malt extract and coconut oil. Whisk gently over the heat to make sure the sugar has fully dissolved.

Stir the chocolate into the mixture until it has melted and the mixture is smooth. Allow to cool completely and blend in the guar or xanthan gum, then give the mixture a final whisk before freezing.

Churn the mixture in an electric ice cream maker, if you have one, according to the manufacturer's instructions until frozen.

Alternatively, freeze the mixture in a shallow container, removing it from the freezer from time to time to give it a whisk. Using the freezer does gives a slightly icy texture - if you don't like this, remove the ice cream from the freezer 10–15 minutes before serving, transfer the mixture to a food processor and pulse for a minute or so until it becomes creamy, then serve immediately.

pecan maple ice cream

You need to allow time for the banana pieces to freeze (and they will keep for a week or so in the freezer), but once that is done this makes a quick and delicious treat for two.

Serves 2

2 small bananas, peeled
10 pecans
4 tbsp maple syrup
a good pinch of salt

Slice the bananas into 2cm (¾in) chunks and place in a single layer on a baking tray. Freeze until solid. You can keep them in the freezer until you are ready to make the ice cream.

Put the frozen banana chunks into a food processor along with half of the nuts, half of the maple syrup and the salt, and process until smooth and creamy.

Chop the remaining nuts and add to the mixture along with the remaining maple syrup, then pulse just a few times to mix lightly. Serve immediately.

*image
p.216–217*

instant coconut maple ice cream with dark chocolate

The coconut milk used here needs to be chilled for several hours – I always keep a couple of cans in my refrigerator so they are ready for immediate use.

Serves 2

1 × 400g (14oz) can full-fat coconut
   milk, refrigerated
2–4 tbsp maple syrup, to taste
grated dark (bittersweet) chocolate,
   to serve

Drain the liquid from the can of coconut milk and discard. Put the solidified coconut cream into a serving bowl and pour the maple syrup on top. Mix lightly, then top with grated chocolate to taste and serve immediately.

*image
p.216–217*

desserts

quick, easy and delicious chocolate brownies

Preheat the oven to 170°C/340°F/gas mark 4.

Line the base and sides of a 20cm (8in) square baking tin (pan) with 2 strips of good-quality non-stick baking paper (so that the bottom has a double layer of paper).

Break the vegan chocolate into pieces and put them into a saucepan along with the vegan butter and sugar. Heat gently until melted, then remove from the heat.

Meanwhile, mix the milk with the vinegar in a bowl and set aside to curdle.

Sift the flour, salt, baking powder and bicarbonate of soda (baking soda) into the chocolate mixture and stir until well combined. Add the curdled milk and mix quickly with a wooden spoon until combined, then thump the pan on the work surface to get rid of any air bubbles. Tip the mixture into the prepared tin, spreading it to the edges, then thump the tin sharply on the surface once again.

Bake for about 20 minutes until firm.

Let cool, then cut into pieces in the tin. The brownies become firmer and fudgier as they cool. They keep well stored in a tin.

These brownies are the result of my many attempts at making 'the perfect vegan brownie'. For me, it's perfect just as it is, but if you want it even more 'fudgy' you can simply double the amount of chocolate and bake the brownies for a few minutes longer. Either way, they are quite delicate when they first come out of the oven, but they soon firm up. In fact, they are even more delicious the next day and keep well... if they are allowed to. I hope you will enjoy them.

Makes 15

100g (3½oz) plain (semisweet) vegan chocolate

100g (3½oz/scant ½ cup) Vegan Butter (see p.266) or vegan spread

125g (4½oz/scant ⅔ cup) soft brown sugar

4 tbsp soy or other plant-based milk

1 tsp cider vinegar or wine vinegar (red or white)

75g (2¾oz/generous ½ cup) self-raising (self-rising) flour

¼ tsp salt

¼ tsp baking powder

½ tsp bicarbonate of soda (baking soda)

baking

SWEET TREATS

In today's hectic world, there are few things more enjoyable than taking a few minutes for yourself and cuddling up with a hot drink and a slice of something sweet to nibble on. Bliss. The recipes for cookies, traybakes and cakes on the following pages offer vegan version of many classic recipes, and are sure to be hit with all of your family and friends.

melt-in-the-mouth shortbread

I'm very grateful to my daughter, Meg, for providing this easy and delicious recipe. These melt-in-the-mouth shortbreads are quick, simple to make and always go down a treat.

Makes 15–20

225g (8oz/1¾ cups) plain (all-purpose) flour
60g (2¼oz/½ cup) icing (confectioners') sugar
150g (5½oz/⅔ cup) vegan margarine
pinch of salt

Preheat the oven to 180°C/350°F/gas mark 4 and grease and line an 18 × 27cm (7 × 11in) Swiss roll tin with baking parchment.

Put all of the ingredients into a bowl or into a food processor. If making by hand, rub the margarine into the dry ingredients with the tips of your fingers until you achieve a breadcrumb consistency, then press the dough together to form a crumbly dough. If using a food processor, simply pulse the ingredients together until a dough forms.

Press the mixture into the prepared tin, spreading it out evenly across the base, then prick all over with a fork. Transfer to the freezer for 20 minutes to chill, then bake for 25–30 minutes until crisp and light golden brown.

Set aside to cool slightly, then cut into pieces while still warm and leave to cool completely in the tin.

best ginger biscuits

These moreish biscuits have a delicious fiery kick and are quick and easy to make with the aid of a food processor.

Preheat the oven to 160°C/325°F/gas mark 3.

Put the flour, bicarbonate of soda (baking soda), ginger, cinnamon, nutmeg and allspice into a food processor and process briefly to combine, then add all the remaining ingredients and process until a soft dough has formed.

Turn the dough out onto a lightly floured surface and roll to a thickness of 5mm (¼in). Using a 7cm (2¾in) circular cookie cutter, stamp out circles and place on a lightly-floured baking sheet. Rerolling the dough and repeating the process until it is all used up. Transfer to the oven and bake for 18–20 minutes, or until firm and light golden.

Leave on the baking sheet to cool and firm up, then carefully remove from the baking sheet using palette knife. Store in an airtight container for up to a week.

note on cookie cutters ...
It can be fun to make these biscuits (cookies) using different shaped cookies cutters – especially if you are cooking with children.

Makes about 20

125g (4½oz/scant 1 cup) plain (all-purpose) flour, plus extra for rolling
¼ tsp bicarbonate of soda (baking soda)
2 tsp ground ginger
¼ tsp ground cinnamon
¼ tsp ground nutmeg
¼ tsp ground allspice
60g (2¼oz/¼ cup) vegan spread
75g (2½oz/generous ⅓ cup) demerara (turbinado) sugar
3 tbsp maple syrup
40g (1½oz) crystallised ginger

image p.225

chocolate chip cookies

Makes about 18 cookies

125g (4½oz/generous ½ cup) vegan
   spread
125g (4½oz/scant ⅔ cup) caster
   (superfine) sugar
200g (7oz/1½ cups) self-raising flour
1 teaspoon baking powder
1 teaspoon vanilla extract
200g (7oz) vegan milk chocolate chips

Preheat the oven to 170°C/340°F/gas mark 3 and line 2
baking sheets with baking parchment.

Put the vegan spread and sugar in a large bowl and
cream together with an electric whisk or wooden spoon
until light and fluffy. Sift in the flour and baking powder,
then add the vanilla, chocolate chips and 1 tablespoon
of water and mix again to form a soft dough.

Using 2 dessert spoons, place spoonfuls of the mixture
on the prepared baking sheets, spacing them evenly
apart to allow the cookies to spread during baking.
Gently flatten the spoonfuls of dough to form small
cookie shapes.

Transfer to the oven and bake for about 12 minutes,
until golden and just starting to firm up. Leave on the
baking sheets for 5 minutes to continue to firm, then
carefully transfer to a wire rack to cool. Store in an airtight
container for up to a week.

golden crunch biscuits

This was one of those recipes that happened by accident when a recipe went wrong but the result was absolutely delicious! They are very quick to make, especially in a food processor.

Makes 15–20 biscuits

150g (5½oz/generous 1 cup) self-raising flour
75g (2½oz/scant ½ cup) semolina
150g (5½oz/⅔ cup) Vegan Butter (p.266) or vegan spread
6 tbsp caster (superfine) sugar

Preheat the oven to 180°C/350°F/gas mark 4 and line an 18 × 27cm (7 × 11in) Swiss roll tin with baking parchment.

Put the flour, semolina, butter or vegan spread and caster (superfine) sugar into a bowl, or food processor, and mix, or process until the mixture begins to clump together.

Press the mixture into the prepared tin, spreading it out evenly across the base, then prick all over with a fork. Bake for for 20 minutes, then remove from the oven and re-prick the top, pressing down the sides if they have risen up above the sides of the tin. Bake for a further 20–25 minutes until the biscuits are a deep golden colour. Slip a knife down the cuts you made to help release the biscuits later, then cool in the tin and remove carefully with a palette knife.

variation

For crunchy ginger biscuits, sift the flour with 1 tsp ground ginger.

flapjacks

Preheat the oven to 190°C/375°F/gas mark 5 and line a 27 × 18cm (7 × 11in) Swiss roll tin or baking sheet with a baking parchment.

Put the sugar, vegan spread and golden (corn) syrup in a pan over a low heat until the butter and sugar have melted, then remove from the heat and stir in the oats.

Pour the mixture onto the prepared Swiss roll tin and allow to spread out into thin layer. Transfer to the oven and cook for 20–25 minutes, until golden brown.

Leave to cool in the tin for 10 minutes, then slice and remove from the tin while they are still warm (they will be very hard to cut if left to completely cool). These will keep in an airtight container for up to a week.

Some of the most popular things have always been secretly vegan: flapjacks for one! I like to make these in a large tin so that they spread out more in the oven, giving a thinner and crisper result.

Makes 12

185g (6½oz/scant 1 cup) dark brown soft sugar
185g (6½oz/generous ¾ cup) Vegan Butter (see p.266) or vegan spread
2 tbsp golden (corn) syrup
175g (6oz/scant 2 cups) rolled oats

millionaire's shortbread

This is an easy recipe for this rich and delicious treat of crisp, melt-in-the mouth shortbread base topped with golden caramel and a layer of chocolate.

To make the shortbread, preheat the oven to 180°C/350°F/gas mark 4. Put the flour, sugar and vegan spread in a large bowl and rub together with your fingertips until a crumbly dough forms. This can also be done by blitzing the mixture in a food processor.

Press the mixture into a 18 × 28cm (7 × 11in) Swiss roll tin, prick the base with a fork, and transfer to the oven to bake for 10–15 minutes, until light golden brown. Set aside to cool.

While the shortbread is cooking, make the caramel. Place a teaspoon in the freezer for testing the caramel later. Without mixing, put all the caramel ingredients in a deep microwavable bowl, then microwave on high for 60 seconds. Remove from the microwave and stir the mixture to form a smooth paste, then return to the microwave for 90 seconds. Stir again, then return the mixture to microwave for a final 90 seconds.

Test the mixture by putting a tiny amount (around ⅛ of a teaspoon) onto the spoon that you put in the freezer earlier. If the mixture quickly begins to set to a soft, pliable consistency, it's done. If the caramel isn't quite ready, microwave for an additional 30 seconds and test again. Once you are happy with the consistency, let the caramel cool and thicken a little, then beat with a wooden spoon for a few minutes until thick. Spread the caramel all over the surface of the cooled shortbread. Leave until it is completely cold and set.

Melt the chocolate in a heatproof bowl set over a pan of boiling water, then spread over the surface of the caramel. Set the shortbread aside until it completely cold and set, then cut into small pieces and serve.

Makes 24 small pieces

For the shortbread:
200g (7oz/1½ cups) plain (all-purpose) flour
50g (1¾oz/¼ cup) caster (superfine) sugar
120g (4¼oz/generous ½ cup) Vegan Butter (see p.266) or vegan spread
pinch of salt

For the caramel:
100g (3½oz/½ cup) caster (superfine) sugar
70g (2½oz/generous ⅓ cup) light brown soft sugar
170g (6oz/scant ⅓ cup) golden (corn) syrup
3 tbsp vegan spread
70g (2½oz) coconut milk powder or barley malt powder

For the chocolate topping:
100g (3½ oz) vegan chocolate (milk or dark, your choice)

scones with jam and cream

Preheat the oven to 200°C/400°F/gas mark 6.

Mix the milk with the lemon juice in a bowl and set aside to curdle.

Sift the flour and baking powder into a bowl – or put them into a food processor – and add the vegan butter or spread. Rub the fat into the flour with your finger-tips until the mixture looks like breadcrumbs, add the sugar, then gradually add the milk and lemon juice mixture and mix to a soft dough – it needs to quite wet but you may not need all of the milk mixture. Do this as quickly as you can while the raising agents are active.

Press the dough out with your hand to a thickness of 4cm (1½ in), then cut into rounds using a 5cm (2in) cutter. Reroll the dough as needed, until you have 8 scones.

Place on a floured baking sheet and bake for around 12 minutes, until risen and firm. Cool on a wire rack.

Serve the scones with jam and vegan whipping cream.

These scones are easy to make, freeze well and thaw quickly – if you warm them in the oven for a few minutes they taste freshly-baked. They are delicious served with jam and vegan whipped 'cream' (see p.267). Eating them instantly transports me back to the wonderful holidays my sister and I spent staying at our great aunt's house in Rock, Cornwall, where we had to be on our best behaviour!

Makes 8 scones

175ml (6fl oz/¾ cup) soya milk
1 tbsp freshly squeezed lemon juice
350g (12oz/2¾ cups) self-raising flour, white or wholemeal (whole wheat)
¼ tsp baking powder
85g (3oz/generous ⅓ cup) Vegan Butter (see p.266) or vegan spread
3 tbsp caster (superfine) sugar
jam and whipped 'cream' (see p.267), to serve

parkin

Preheat the oven to 180°C/350°F/gas mark 4. Grease a deep 20cm (8in) square tin (pan) and line with baking parchment.

Sift the flour, baking powder and ginger into a large bowl, then add the oatmeal and set aside.

Put the sugar, treacle, syrup and vegan spread into a pan over a gentle heat and stir until everything has melted. Set aside to cool for 5 minutes, then stir in the plant milk. Pour this mixture into the flour mixture and stir well to combine.

Pour the mixture into the prepared cake tin (pan), transfer to the oven and bake for 50–60 minutes, until firm to the touch. Cool in the tin for 10 minutes, then turn out and transfer to a wire rack until completely cooled. Cut into 12 pieces and serve.

This is a type of gingerbread that gets more sticky and delicious the longer it's kept. It's a traditional recipe much loved by my Yorkshire-born Dad, and a recipe that I have given before in my *Complete Vegetarian Cookbook*, but it is so quick and easy to make, and so good to eat, that I wanted to supply a vegan version here, too.

Makes 12 pieces

125g (4½oz/scant 1 cup) plain (all-purpose) or wholemeal (whole wheat) flour
2 tsp baking powder
2 tsp ground ginger
125g (4½oz/scant 1 cup) medium oatmeal
75g (2½oz/generous ⅓ cup) light brown soft sugar
125g (4½oz/generous ⅓ cup) black treacle
125g (4½oz/generous ⅓ cup) golden (corn) syrup
125g (4½oz/generous ½ cup) Vegan Butter (see p.266) or vegan spread
175ml (6fl oz/scant ¾ cup) plant milk

gingerbread

Preheat the oven to 160°C/325°F/gas mark 3 and line a deep 20cm (8in) square tin (pan) with baking parchment

Mix the milk with the lemon juice in a bowl and set aside to curdle.

Put the syrup, treacle, sugar and olive oil in a pan over a moderate heat and stir until melted, then set aside to cool for five minutes.

Meanwhile, sift the flour, ground ginger, baking powder, bicarbonate of soda (baking soda) and salt into a bowl, then stir in the syrup mixture from the pan. Add the curdled milk and mix quickly with a wooden spoon until combined, then thump the pan on the work surface to get rid of any air bubbles. Tip the mixture into the prepared tin, spreading it to the edges, then thump the tin sharply on the surface once again.

Transfer to the oven to bake for 45–50 minutes, until well risen and firm to the touch. Leave to cool in the tin for 15 minutes, then turn out onto a wire rack, strip off the paper and leave to cool completely before slicing. Store for up to a week in an airtight tin.

My mother used to rustle up gingerbread for any family occasion: a picnic by the sea in summer; watching fireworks round a bonfire in the winter; Christmas ... She often used to make two large slabs, putting one away in a tin for a week to get nice and sticky (though it usually didn't last that long).

Makes 16 bite-sized pieces

200ml (7fl oz/scant 1 cup) plant milk
4 tsp freshly squeezed lemon juice
50g (1¾oz/⅛ cup) golden (corn) syrup
150g (5½oz/scant ½ cup) black treacle
100g (3½oz/½ cup) light brown
    soft sugar
5 tbsp light coloured olive oil
200g (7oz/1½ cups) self-raising flour
1 tsp ground ginger
¼ tsp baking powder
¼ tsp bicarbonate of soda
    (baking soda)
¼ tsp salt

celebration cupcakes

Preheat the oven to 180°C/350°F/gas mark 4 and line a 12-hole cupcake tin with paper cases.

Mix the milk with the lemon juice in a bowl and set aside to curdle.

Sift the flour, salt, bicarbonate of soda (baking soda) and baking powder into a bowl, add the caster (superfine) sugar and vegan butter or spread and beat with a wooden spoon or electric beaters until well combined.

Add the curdled milk and mix quickly with a wooden spoon until combined, then thump the pan on the work surface to get rid of any air bubbles. Spoon the mixture into the prepared muffin cases, then thump the cupcake tin sharply on the surface once again.

Transfer to the oven to bake for 15–20 minutes, until risen and firm. Set aside to cool in the tin.

To make the buttercream, put all of the ingredients into a large bowl and beat together with an electric beater for 4–5 minutes, until smooth and glossy.

When the cakes are completely cold, top each with a good swirl of butter cream – you can use a spoon or a piping bag for this, then decorate as you wish.

Makes 12

150ml (5fl oz/generous ½ cup) soy, almond or oat milk
4 tsp freshly-squeezed lemon juice
150g (5½oz/generous 1 cup) self-raising flour
¼ tsp salt
¼ tsp bicarbonate of soda (baking soda)
¼ tsp baking powder
110g (4oz/generous ½ cup) caster (superfine) sugar
75g (2½oz/⅓ cup) Vegan Butter (see p.266) or vegan spread

For the buttercream:
500g (1lb 2oz/generous 3½ cups) icing sugar
85g (3oz/generous ⅓ cup) vegan spread, at room temperature
6 tbsp soya milk
1 tsp vanilla extract

chocolate and ginger rock cakes

My mother used to rustle up rock cakes and pop them into the Aga literally as visitors walked up the garden. They made the house smell so welcoming and were delicious eaten warm from the oven.

Makes 8

200g (7oz/1½ cups) self-raising flour
1 tsp ground ginger
100g (3½oz/scant ½ cup) Vegan Butter (see p.266) or vegan spread
75g (2½oz/generous ⅓ cup) caster (superfine) sugar
50g (1¾oz/⅓ cup) vegan dark chocolate chips, or chopped dark chocolate
75g (2¾oz) crystallised ginger, roughly chopped
1–2 tbsp water

Preheat the oven to 200°C/400°F/gas mark 6 and line a baking sheet with baking parchment.

Sift the flour and ground ginger into a large bowl or electric mixer, then add the vegan spread. Rub the butter into the dry ingredients until the mixture resembles breadcrumbs, or, if using an electric mixer, process until you achieve a breadcrumb consistency. Mix in the sugar, chocolate chips and ginger, then add enough water to just bring the mixture together.

Using 2 dessert spoons, place spoonfuls of the mixture on the prepared baking sheets, spacing them evenly apart to allow the rock cakes to spread during baking. Bake for about 15 minutes, until golden brown. Leave to cool on the baking sheet for 5 minutes, then transfer to a wire rack to cool, or eat warm from the oven if you prefer.

rich fruit cake

This wonderful fruit cake is delicious eaten just as it is, but it's also very special when covered in almond paste and icing for a celebration.

Preheat the oven to 160°C/320°F/gas mark 3. Grease a 20cm (8in) tin (pan) with vegan spread and line with 2 layers of baking parchment.

Mix the milk with the lemon juice in a bowl and set aside to curdle.

Beat the vegan butter or spread with the sugar and orange rind in a large bowl until light and fluffy, then sift in the flour, baking powder, bicarbonate of soda (baking soda) and salt, and add the dried fruit and ground almonds.

Gently stir the mixture with a wooden spoon, until just combined, then quickly pour the milk and lemon juice mixture into the bowl and stir again to combine. Tap the bowl sharply on the work surface to pop and bubbles and stop the mixture from rising too quickly, then spoon the mixture into prepared cake tin (pan) and scatter the flaked (slivered) almonds over the top.

Transfer to the oven and bake for 1 hour 30–1 hour 40 minutes, until well risen and a skewer inserted into the cake comes out clean.

Cool the cake completely in the tin, then turn out and remove the paper. Store the cake in an airtight tin until ready to slice.

Makes one 20cm (8in) cake, serving 6–8

150ml (5fl oz/generous ½ cup) plant milk
juice of ½ lemon juice
175g (6oz/generous ¾ cup) Vegan Butter (see p.266) or vegan spread
175g (6oz/generous ¾ cup) light brown soft sugar
grated zest and juice of 1 orange
300g (10½oz/2¼ cups) plain (all-purpose) flour
¼ tsp baking powder
¼ tsp bicarbonate of soda (baking soda)
¼ tsp salt
350g (12oz) mixed dried fruit, soaked for 30 minutes in the juice from the orange
75g (2½oz/½ cup) glacé cherries, halved
50g (1¾oz/½ cup) ground almonds
25g (1oz/⅓ cup) flaked (slivered) almonds

really decadent chocolate cake

This is a big, voluptuous chocolate cake with a glossy, fudgy icing. It's a real showstopper and makes the perfect cake for any celebration or special occasion.

Makes one 20cm (8in) cake

350ml (12fl oz/scant 1½ cups) plant milk
1½ tbsp freshly-squeezed lemon juice
250g (9oz/generous 1¾ cups) self-raising flour
½ tsp baking powder
½ tsp bicarbonate of soda (baking soda)
30g (1oz) cocoa powder
250g (9oz/1¼ cups) caster (superfine) sugar
6 tbsp light olive oil or rapeseed oil
75g (2¾oz) dark vegan chocolate, melted
1 tbsp vanilla essence

For the icing and filling:
500g (1lb 2oz/generous 3½ cups) icing sugar
80g (2¾oz) cocoa powder
85g (3oz/generous ⅓ cup) Vegan Butter (see p.266) or vegan spread
6 tbsp soya milk
115g (4oz) dark vegan chocolate, melted

Preheat the oven to 180°C/350°F/gas mark 4. Lightly grease two 20cm (8in) cake tins (pans) and line the bases with baking parchment.

Mix the milk with the lemon juice in a bowl and set aside to curdle.

Sift the flour, baking powder, bicarbonate of soda (baking soda) and cocoa powder into a large bowl. Add the caster (superfine) sugar, oil, melted chocolate, vanilla essence and the soy milk and lemon mixture, and beat with a wooden spoon or electric mixer until smooth and glossy. Tap the bowl sharply on the work surface to dispel any air bubbles and stop the mixture rising too quickly, then divide the mixture between the cake tins.

Transfer to the oven and bake for 25–30 minutes, until well risen and firm to the touch.

Cool the cakes in the tin for 10 minutes, then turn out and transfer to a wire rack to cool completely.

While the cakes are cooling, make the icing by putting all of the ingredients in a bowl and beating with an electric whisk for 4–5 minutes, until smooth and glossy.

To assemble the cake, spoon half the icing on top of one of the cakes and spread out to almost cover, then top with the other cake. Spoon the remaining icing on top of the cake and spread to cover.

lemon drizzle cake

Makes 1 × 900g (2lb) loafcake

200ml (7fl oz/generous ¾ cup) soy, almond or oat milk

zest and juice of 2 lemons

200g (7oz/1½ cups) self-raising flour

¼ tsp salt

¼ tsp bicarbonate of soda (baking soda)

¼ tsp baking powder

200g (7oz/1 cup) caster (superfine) sugar

5 tbsp lightly-flavoured olive oil or rapeseed oil

150g (5½oz/1 cup) icing (confectioners') sugar

Preheat the oven to 160°C/325°F/gas mark 3 and line a 900g (2lb) loaf tin with lightly greased baking parchment.

Mix the milk with ¼ of the lemon juice in a bowl and set aside to curdle.

Sift the flour, salt, bicarbonate of soda (baking soda) and baking powder into a bowl, then add the caster (superfine) sugar, lemon zest, oil, and the milk and lemon mixture.

Working quickly, stir the mixture with a wooden spoon for not more than 10 seconds – it is important not to over-mix. Tap the bowl once sharply on the work surface to dispel any air bubbles and prevent the mixture from rising too quickly.

Spoon the mixture into the prepared tin, tap again on the work surface to get rid of air bubbles, then transfer to the oven to bake for 30–35 minutes, or until risen, firm to the touch and an inserted skewer inserted comes out clean.

Once the cake is out of the oven, combine the icing (confectioner's) sugar and the remaining lemon juice in a bowl and stir until smooth and lump free. Prick the top of the cake all over with a skewer, pour the icing over it, and allow it to seep into the cake.

Once the cake has completely cooled, remove from the tin, slice and serve.

sponge cake with jam and cream

This is a beautiful light sponge cake that can be filled with jam and dredged with a little caster (superfine) sugar, or filled and topped with buttercream.

Makes one 18cm (7in) cake

150ml (5fl oz/generous ½ cup) soy, almond or oat milk
juice of ½ lemon
150g (5½oz/generous 1 cup) self-raising flour
¼ tsp salt
¼ tsp bicarbonate of soda (baking soda)
¼ tsp baking powder
110g (4oz/scant ¾ cup) caster (superfine) sugar, plus extra, to dust (optional)
75g (2½oz/⅓ cup) Vegan Butter (see p.266) or vegan spread
jam of your choice, to fill
½ quantity vanilla buttercream (see p.235), to fill

Preheat the oven to 180°C/350°F/gas mark 4 and line a 18cm (7in) cake tin (pan) with lightly greased baking parchment.

Mix the milk with the lemon juice in a bowl and set aside to curdle.

Sift the flour, salt, bicarbonate of soda (baking soda) and baking powder into a bowl, add the caster (superfine) sugar and vegan spread and mix with a wooden spoon until well combined. Working quickly, pour in the milk and lemon juice mixture and stir quickly to combine, being careful not to overwork the mixture. Tap the bowl sharply on the work surface to dispel any air bubbles and prevent the mixture from rising too quickly.

Spoon the mixture into the prepared tins (pans), tap them again on the work surface, then transfer to the oven for 25–30 minutes, until risen, firm to the light touch and an inserted skewer comes out clean.

When completely cool, remove the cake from the tin, strip off the baking parchment and slice in half horizontally.

Spoon a generous layer of jam onto one of the cake layers and top with the buttercream, spreading almost to the edges of the cake, then top with the other layer of cake and press down gently. Dust the cake with a little extra caster sugar, if you like, then slice and serve.

miracle meringues

These are made from the liquid strained from canned chick peas, named 'aquafaba'. Amazingly, it whisks up just like egg white, and it can then be made into the most delectable meringues. You've got to try this!

Preheat the oven to 100°C/210°F/gas mark ¼ and line 2 baking sheets with baking parchment.

In a large, grease-free bowl with an electric mix, or the bowl of a stand mixer, whisk the aquafaba for 10 minutes, until the mixture has stiff peaks. Add the vinegar and whisk for one minute more, then start adding the sugar, very slowly, 1 tablespoon at a time, whipping well between each addition.

Once all the sugar has been used up and the meringue is smooth, stiff and glossy, spoon or pipe 8 equal-sized meringues onto the prepared baking sheets, then transfer to the oven to bake for 2 hours. After this time, turn off the oven and open the door slightly, but leave the meringues inside for a further 45–60 minutes.

Test the meringues are done by tapping the bases – they should be dry to the touch and sound hollow. The meringues can be used straightaway or kept in an airtight container for up to a week.

Bake for 2 hours, then turn off the oven and leave meringues inside with oven door open slightly for a further ¾–1 hour. Make sure they are very dry and sound hollow when you tap the base. Use straightaway or transfer to an airtight container for up to a week, until ready to use.

To make the coconut whipped cream, scoop the hard, thickened coconut cream from the top of the cans into a large bowl, being careful not to add any thinner liquid. Add the icing (confectioners') sugar and vanilla extract, and whisk with an electric beater for about 2 minutes, until fluffy. Refrigerate for 30 minutes before using.

Serve the meringues topped with coconut whipped cream and the fruit of your choice.

Makes 8 large meringues

120ml (4fl oz/½ cup) aquafaba (the strained liquid from a 400g tin chickpeas)
½ tsp white or red wine vinegar
125g (4½oz/scant ⅔ cup) caster (superfine) sugar
fresh fruit, to serve

For the coconut whipped cream:
2 × 400g (14oz) cans full-fat coconut milk, chilled overnight
100g (3½oz/scant ¾ cup) icing (confectioners') sugar, sifted
1 tsp vanilla extract

BREAD

Homemade bread is an absolute joy and deceptively simple to make. Most of the bread you buy is vegan, but I couldn't resist adding a couple of my favourite everyday loaves to the baking section of this book.

bread rolls

Pre-heat the oven to 220°C/425°F/gas mark 7 and line two baking sheets with baking parchment.

Put the flour and yeast into a large mixing bowl and mix well to distribute the yeast. Add the salt and sugar and mix again to combine. Make a well in the centre of the flour and pour in the milk and butter, then gradually incorporate the flour into the soy milk to form a dough.

Turn the dough out onto a floured work surface and knead for 10–15 minutes, until the dough is elastic, smooth and no longer sticky. Transfer to a clean, lightly oiled bowl, cover with cling film (plastic wrap) and set aside at room temperature for 1–2 hours, until almost doubled in size.

Transfer the dough to a lightly dusted work surface. Gently press into a long rectangle, fold each of the long edges towards the centre, then fold onto itself into a long sausage. Cut into 12 equal pieces. Flatten each piece, lightly fold the edges towards the centre, turn around, roll with your hand to shape into a perfect round ball. Lay the balls on the baking sheets, cover and leave for another hour until doubled in size.

Using a sharp knife, make a couple of slashes on top of the buns. Brush with a little soy milk, transfer to the oven and bake for 5 minutes, then lower the temperature to 200°C/400°F/gas mark 6 for 10 more minutes until golden brown. Leave to cool on a wire rack.

Makes 24 small rolls

750g (1lb 10oz/6¼ cups) strong white bread flour
1 × 7g sachet easy-bake yeast
80g (3oz) vegan spread
4 tsp sugar
2 tsp pink salt
About 450ml (16fl oz/scant 2 cups) soy milk (or any plant based milk), plus extra for glazing
vegetable oil for greasing

wholemeal loaf

Pre-heat the oven to 200°C/400°F/gas mark 6 and grease 1 large (900g/2lb) or 2 small (450g/1lb) loaf pans with oil or vegan spread.

Put the flour, yeast and salt into a large mixing bowl and mix well to distribute. Make a well in the centre of the flour and pour in the water, then gradually incorporate the flour into the water to form a smooth dough that leaves the sides of the bowl clean.

If you are making a single loaf, stretch the dough out into a rectangle, then fold the sides under and put into the prepared pan, with the seam in the dough underneath. Push the corners of the loaf down slightly to emphasise the dome of the loaf.

If making 2 smaller loaves, divide the dough into 2 equal pieces and proceed as above.

Scatter the loaf with a little flour, then transfer the tin to a large polythene bag and leave undisturbed until well risen, with the centre of the loaf higher than the sides of the tin.

Once risen, transfer the tin(s) to the oven and cook for 40 minutes, until golden, well risen and hollow-sounding when tapped underneath.

Transfer to a wire rack to cool before serving.

This is the wholemeal bread that my sister and I were brought up on, and which, when it appeared in our lunch boxes, was an object of wonder and amazement to all the other children. It's versatile, easy to make – especially with the easy blend yeast that you can buy today – and delicious. I've adapted the recipe from one in my very first book, *Simply Delicious*, which was published in 1966, and it still tastes as good today as it did back then.

Makes 1 large or 2 small loaves

450g (1lb/scant 3½ cups) wholemeal (whole wheat) flour, preferably stone ground
1 × 7g sachet (2 tsp) easy-bake yeast
2 tsp salt
350ml (12fl oz/scant 1½ cups) warm water
oil or vegan spread, for greasing

basic white loaf

This is a very easy, basic bread dough; it makes a lovely loaf, or the perfect base for a homemade pizza; it's also great for rolls.

Pre-heat the oven to 220°C/425°F/gas mark 7 and line a baking sheet with baking parchment.

Put both flours, the yeast and salt into a large mixing bowl and mix well to distribute. Make a well in the centre of the flour and pour in the water and olive oil, then gradually incorporate the flour into the soy milk to form a dough.

Turn the dough out onto a floured work surface and knead for 10–15 minutes, until the dough is elastic, smooth and no longer sticky. Transfer to a clean, lightly oiled bowl, cover with cling film (plastic wrap) and set aside at room temperature for 1–2 hours, until almost doubled in size.

Gently knock back the dough and mould into a ball. Place on the prepared baking sheet and set aside for about 45 minutes, or until doubled in size.

Slash the top of the loaf with a sharp knife and dust the top with flour. Transfer to the oven and bake for 10 minutes, then lower the oven temperature to 200°C/400°F/gas mark 6 and bake for 35–40 minutes more, until well risen and golden brown. To test if done, turn over and tap the base, it should sound like a hollow drum.

Transfer to a wire rack to cool before serving.

250g (9oz/generous 2 cups) strong white bread flour
250g (9oz/generous 2 cups) plain (all-purpose) flour
1½ tsp easy blend dried yeast
1 tsp salt
300ml (10fl oz/1¼ cups) warm water
1 tbsp olive oil
extra flour, for dusting

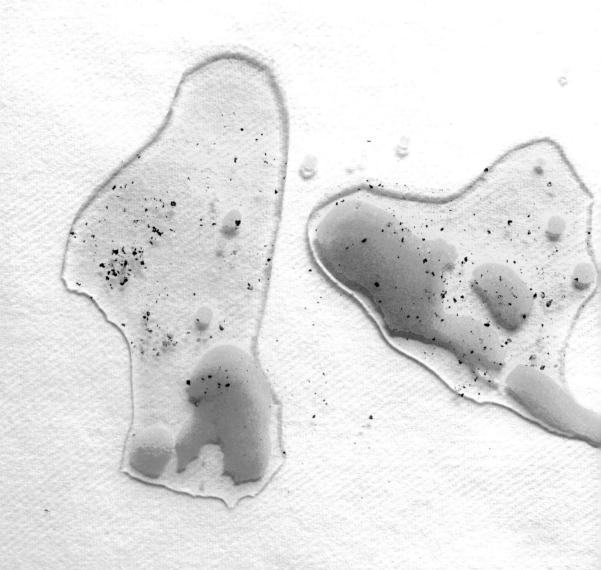

basics

GRAVIES, SAUCES & DRESSINGS

Whether you are making
a simple salad, a Sunday roast
or even a delicious pudding,
sometimes all you need is
a simple sauce or dressing
as a final flourish to bring
a dish together.

my mother's onion gravy

My mother was famous for her delicious gravy. The recipe makes a generous amount, but everyone loves it, and if there's any over, it will keep well for a few days in the fridge or can be frozen until needed.

Put the olive oil in a medium pan over a high heat. Once hot, add the onions to the pan and turn the heat to low. Cook, stirring occasionally, for 10–15 minutes, until the onions are soft and just starting to turn golden.

Add the flour to the pan and stir for a couple of minutes to coat the onions and cook off the flour, then gradually add the stock, stirring between additions to thicken with the onion and flour mixture.

Once all of the water has been added, blend the mixture with a hand (immersion) blender, until smooth. Then stir in the marmite and add the shoyu or soy sauce to taste. soy sauce to add colour and flavour. Leave to cook for a couple of minutes more to allow the flavours to develop, then serve.

Serves 4

2 tbsp olive oil
1 onion, peeled and finely chopped
2–3 tbsp plain (all-purpose) flour
800ml (1⅓ pints/3⅓ cups) hot
    vegetable stock
2 tsp yeast extract (I use Marmite)
shoyu or soy sauce, to taste

red pepper sauce

Combine the (bell) peppers, garlic and water in a saucepan and simmer over a gentle heat for about 15 minutes, or until the pepper is very tender. If you want a slightly thicker sauce, add the cornflour (cornstarch) mixture and stir over the heat for a few further minutes. Transfer to a food processor or use a hand-held stick blender to process to a smooth purée.

You can make this sauce with the water drained from cooking vegetables, such as celeriac (see p.154), made up to the desired quantity with some boiling water if necessary. You can also add ½ teaspoon of stock (bouillon) powder, for extra flavour.

Serves 4–6

2 large red (bell) peppers, deseeded and sliced
2 garlic cloves, peeled
300ml (10fl oz/1¼ cups) hot water or vegetable cooking water
1 tsp cornflour (cornstach) mixed with a little cold water, to thicken (optional)

quick parsley sauce

Serves 4–6

25g (1oz) Vegan Butter (see p.266) or vegan spread
25g (1oz) plain (all-purpose) flour
600ml (20fl oz/2½ cups) plant milk of your choice
1 tbsp chopped fresh parsley
sea salt and freshly ground black pepper, to taste

Place the butter or spread in a saucepan over a low heat to melt. Once melted, add the flour to the pan and stir for a couple of minutes to thicken and cook off the flour. Remove the pan from the heat and gradually add in the milk, stirring between additions to thicken slightly. Return the pan to the heat and cook, stirring, over a low heat for a couple of minutes until the sauce is smooth, glossy and coats the back of a spoon. Season with salt and pepper to taste, stir in the chopped parsley and serve hot.

note

This can also be made quickly by placing all of the ingredients into a food processor or liquidizer, substituting the flour for 15g (½ oz) cornflour (cornstarch) and adding whole sprigs of parsley, rather than chopped. Process the mixture until smooth, then transfer to a pan and cook over a low heat for a couple of minutes until smooth and thickened.

easy balsamic dressing

This is the basic dressing that I always have ready to go in my fridge. It's the work of moments and always makes even the simplest plate of salad leaves feel just a bit special.

Makes enough 1–2 large bowls of salad

Put the mustard, salt, balsamic vinegar and olive oil into a small jar and shake until combined. Add a pinch of two of caster sugar, or, even nicer, ½-1 tsp of maple syrup to taste. This is lovely when freshly made but will also keep in the fridge for 7–10 days or so, just refresh the dressing by giving the dressing a quick shake before using.

½ tsp Dijon mustard
½ tsp salt
1 tbsp balsamic vinegar (check that it's vegan)
3 tbsp olive oil
caster (superfine) sugar or maple syrup, to taste

garlic tofu mayonnaise

This is a beautifully thick sauce that is halfway between a dressing and a mayonnaise. The addition of tofu makes this a great way of adding a hit of protein to a simple salad.

Simply place all of the ingredients in a blender or food processor and blend until beautifully smooth.

200g (7oz) silken tofu
2 garlic cloves, crushed (optional)
1 tsp caster (superfine) sugar (optional)
sea salt, to taste

vegan mayo

Put all of the ingredients into a deep, flat-based jug or basin suitable for use with a hand (immersion) blender – this works best when jug or basin is roughly the same circumference as the head of the hand (immersion) blender.

Blend the mixture for a few moments, until the ingredients come together into a beautifully thick and creamy mayonnaise. Adjust the seasoning if necessary, then serve.

variations

Aioli: To make a beautifully garlicy aioli, simply add a crushed clove of garlic with the other ingredients and proceed as above.

Tartare Sauce: To make a tartare sauce, stir 2 tablespoons chopped capers, 2 tablespoons chopped gherkins, 1 tablespoon chopped chives and 1 tablespoon chopped parsley into the finished mayonnaise.

You really don't need eggs to make the most fabulous mayonnaise, and, with an electric hand (immersion) blender it can be made in an instant. Although I prefer olive oil for most of my cooking, rapeseed oil works best for this – I like to use an organic one. Key here is to make sure that all the ingredients are at room temperature before you start. This keeps in the fridge for 7–10 days.

Makes about 150ml (5fl oz/generous ½ cup)

220ml (8fl oz/scant 1 cup) organic rapeseed oil, at room temperature
120ml (4fl oz/½ cup) unsweetened soy, oat, or almond milk, at room temperature
1 tsp Dijon mustard, at room temperature
1–2 tsp cider or red/white wine vinegar, at room temperature
½ tsp salt
generous pinch kala namak (optional)

butterscotch sauce

Put the butter or spread, both sugars and golden (corn syrup) in a pan over a low heat and cook, stirring occasionally, until the butter and sugar has melted. Continue to cook for another 5 minutes, then remove from the heat and stir in the soya cream and vanilla essence. Serve warm or cooled.

This unctuously sweet sauce will transform a simple bowl of vegan vanilla ice cream into a real celebration dessert. The inspiration for this came from a Delia Smith recipe that I decided to try and veganise one day with great success. It will keep in a jar in the fridge for several weeks.

Serves 4

50g (1¾oz) Vegan Butter (see p.266) or vegan spread
75g (2½oz/generous ⅓ cup) brown sugar
50g (1¾oz/¼ cup) granulated sugar
150g (5½oz/scant ½ cup) golden (corn) syrup
100ml (3½fl oz/scant ½ cup) soya cream
¼ tsp vanilla essence

THE VEGAN DAIRY

The one thing I hear new (or even long-standing!) vegans struggling with most is the lack of cheese in the vegan diet. Traditionally, it has been hard to replicate the salty-umami taste of 'real' cheese from plant-based ingredients, but in recent years vegan products have come on leaps and bounds and there is now a myriad of delicious vegan cheese on the market. It is also relatively simple to make wonderful vegan cheeses at home, as the recipes on the following pages will demonstrate. Not just wonderful to cook with, these would also make a wonderful hostess gift to a vegan dinner party, too. This section also contains recipes for a wonderful vegan butter and easy home-made nut milk, too.

'cheese' sauce

Makes about 600ml (20fl oz/2½ cups)

450g (1lb) floury potatoes, peeled and
    diced into 2.5cm (1 in) chunks
225g (8oz) carrots, peeled and sliced
    into 5mm (¼ in) rounds
100ml (3½fl oz/scant ½ cup) olive oil
1½ tsp salt
1–2 tbsp lemon juice
40g (1½oz) nutritional yeast
½ tsp onion granules
½ tsp garlic powder

Put the potatoes and carrots in a large pan and cover with water. Bring to the boil over a high heat, then reduce to a simmer and leave to cook for 15–20 minutes, until tender. Drain through a colander, leave to steam dry for a couple of minutes and then transfer the vegetables to a blender.

Add the remaining ingredients to the blender, then blend on high speed until smooth and velvety.

note on volume ...

This makes a large volume of sauce, so do scale the recipe up or down to suit your needs.

melting 'cheese'

Place the potatoes in a saucepan, cover with water and boil until tender, about 15 minutes.

Drain, then transfer the potatoes to a food processor. Add the coconut oil, salt, lemon juice, nutritional yeast, onion and garlic powders and process until very smooth (this is important; you do not want any lumps).

Pour the mixture into a suitable container and leave to cool, then chill in the refrigerator for at least an hour until firm.

This makes a cheese with a consistency rather like mozzarella, firm enough to be cut into slices, but not firm enough for grating. It tastes delicious, sliced and eaten as it is – lovely on crackers or in sandwiches. It can also be cooked, on top of pizza or toast for instance, where it does not melt exactly but will soften and brown a little, giving a very pleasant effect. I love it! It also freezes well, so you can make a big batch and save some in the freezer for later.

Makes about 300g (10½oz)

250g (9oz) potatoes, peeled and diced
50g (2oz/¼ cup) coconut oil, melted
1 tsp salt
2 tsp fresh lemon juice
15g (½oz/¼ cup) nutritional yeast
    flakes
¼ tsp onion powder
¼ tsp garlic powder

cream 'cheese'

This is gorgeous and so easy to make. It is great plain but would make a lovely inclusion to a vegan cheese board with the addition of crushed garlic and chives, or perhaps rolled in crushed black pepper.

Put the cashew nuts in a bowl, cover with cold water and leave to soak for 1–2 hours.

Drain the nuts, reserving the liquid. Transfer the nuts with 6 tablespoons of the reserved soaking liquid to a food processor with the lemon juice and garlic, if using, then process until really smooth and creamy, adding more water in necessary.

Stir in a little salt to taste, then add the chopped chives, if using. This can be served as it is, spread on crackers or as a dip for crudités, or formed into balls and rolled in a little black pepper to make a lovely addition to a vegan cheese board.

Serves 2–4

150g (5½oz/generous 1 cup)
    raw unsalted cashew nuts
juice of ½ lemon
1 garlic clove, crushed (optional)
1 tbsp chopped chives (optional)
freshly ground pepper (optional)
sea salt, to taste

'parmesan'

I'd be lying if I said that this tasted exactly like Parmesan cheese, but it's a great alternative, offers the same salty tang and I love it! Don't expect a solid block when making this, this makes a deliciously cheesy rubble that is perfect for scattering over a vegan lasagne or pizza before baking.

Place all the ingredients in a food processor and blend to a 'mealy' texture. Taste and adjust the seasoning if necessary, adding more salt or garlic powder as required. This keeps in a covered container in the fridge for up to two weeks.

100g (3½oz/¾ cup) Brazil nuts
2 tbsp pine nuts
1 tbsp hemp seeds
15g (½ oz/¼ cup) nutritional yeast
¾ tsp sea salt
¼ tsp garlic powder (optional)

mozzarella-style 'cheese'

This 'cheese' and its variations (listed below) make a wonderfully impressive vegan cheeseboard to finish a meal. They can also be used in your cooking as you would use traditional mozzarella.

Makes 1 large mozzarella-style cheese

80g (3oz/scant ¾ cup) raw unsalted cashew nuts

4 tbsp melted coconut oil

4 tbsp tapioca flour

1 tbsp nutritional yeast flakes

1½ tbsp kappa carrageenan (red seaweed extract, used as binding agent)

1 tbsp lemon juice

1½ tsp salt

Have ready a heat-proof dish or mould that will comfortably contain a volume of 750ml (1¼ pints/ generous 3 cups) liquid. This will be the mould for the cheese, so a round dish would work well.

Put the cashews into a bowl, cover with boiling water, and set aside for five minutes to soften slightly.

Drain the cashews and put them into a blender, followed by all the other ingredients and 375ml (13fl oz/generous 1½ cups) boiling water. Put the lid on the blender and blend until completely smooth. You may need to stop the blender and scrape down the sides, then resume blending, until perfectly smooth.

Quickly tip the mixture into your dish or mould before it starts to set, then transfer to the fridge for 2–3 hours to chill and firm up.

Once chilled, tip the cheese out of its mould and pat dry with kitchen paper to remove any excess moisture, then wrap in clingfilm (plastic wrap) or greaseproof paper and store in the fridge until ready to use.

variations

DOUBLE GLOUCESTER WITH CHIVES: Add 2 teaspoon of tomato purée (paste), 1 teaspoon of cider vinegar and 3 tablespoons of chopped chives to the mixture before blending.

BLUE CHEESE: Add 1 tablespoon of white miso paste, half a teaspoon of onion powder, quarter of a teaspoon of garlic powder and 1 teaspoon of lactic acid powder to the mixture before blending. After blending gently stir through quarter–half a teaspoon of spirulina powder to achieve a 'marble' effect similar to blue cheese.

265

nut milk

Makes 750ml (1¼ pints/generous 3 cups)

There are many plant alternatives to dairy milk and they are widely available, but you can also make your own too, using almonds, sunflower seeds or hulled hemp seeds. Volume measurements are best for this as they are easy to scale up and down if you keep the proportions the same – it doesn't' necessarily have to be a standard cup. You can strain the milk through clean sheets of muslin but, if you are going to make nut milk at home regularly, it may be worth investing in a nut milk bag.

Blend the nuts or seeds with the water in a food processor or liquidizer on high. Pour the mixture through a clean sheet of muslin or a nut bag set over a bowl. Once all the liquid has strained through, squeeze the muslin sheet or bag to release any more liquid. Transfer the sealable bottle and store in the fridge for up to 3 days before using.

1 cup almonds, sunflower seeds or hulled hemp seeds (hemp seedesd that have had their outer coating removed)
3 cups water
2 soaked dates or a dash of maple syrup
a few drops of vanilla essence, optional

vegan butter

500ml (18fl oz/generous 2 cups) refined coconut oil, melted
120 ml (4 fl oz/½ cup) vegan milk
4 tbsp light olive oil
½ tsp salt
2 tsp liquid lecithin

To make the butter, simply put all the ingredients into a blender or food processor and blend until well combined. Transfer the mixture to ramekins or a butter dish and leave to set in the fridge until ready to use.

whipped 'cream'

Makes about 240ml (9fl oz/1 cup)

250ml (9fl oz/scant 1 cup) light olive oil (light in colour and flavour, not low fat!), at room temperature
4–8 tbsp unsweetened soya, almond or oat milk, at room temperature
1½–2 tsp caster (superfine) sugar, to taste
1–2 tsp vanilla extract (optional)

This recipe results in a cream very similar to thick whipped double cream. You do need a stick (immersion) blender, but the method is really quick and easy. The less plant milk you use, the thicker the cream will be but, after whisking, you can thin it down if necessary. You can also turn it into sour cream by adding a little lemon juice (see variation, below). The olive oil and the plant milk – one of the thicker ones, soy, almond or oat – must be at room temperature for this to work.

Put the olive oil and plant milk into the goblet of a high-powered immersion blender – I use a hand one – and blend at top speed until the mixture thickens to the texture of whipped double cream, this should happen quite quickly. When you are happy with the consistency, gently stir in the caster (superfine) sugar and vanilla extract, if using.

variation

SOUR CREAM: To make a delicious sour cream, follow the recipe as above, ommiting the caster (superfine) sugar and vanilla extract, then stir in 2–4 tsp of lemon juice or cider vinegar to 'sour' the cream. Season with a little salt, to taste, then serve.

note on cream ...

A quick alternative to this whipped double cream is the Coconut Whipped Cream on p.244.

For single cream, there are many good options available to buy in stores. I like Alpro's single soy cream.

SPICE BOX

A little bit of spice can transform a dish from bland and uninteresting to a flavor-packed feast for the senses. Make up a batch of any of the spice mixes below to add some instant sunshine to your food.

za'atar

To make this delicious spicy, Middle-Eastern topping, simply toast 2 tablespoons sesame seeds in a dry pan for a couple of minutes, until they smell 'toasty' and begin to turn a slightly deeper colour. Remove from the heat and whiz briefly in an electric coffee grinder, then mix with ½ teaspoon sea salt (or pink Himalayan salt), 2 teaspoons ground sumac (a delicious spice that you can buy from Middle Eastern stores), and 2 tablespoons chopped fresh thyme. Sprinkle over the hummus, or serve it in a bowl for people to help themselves.

ras el hanout

You can buy this popular Moroccan flavouring, or you can make it yourself by mixing together: 1½ teaspoons ground coriander seeds, 1¼ teaspoons ground cinnamon, 1 teaspoon paprika, ¾ teaspoon cumin seeds, ½ teaspoon crushed chilli flakes, ½ teaspoon ground cardamom, ½ teaspoon ground ginger and ½ teaspoon ground turmeric.

gomasio

This Japanese sesame salt is easy to make and delicious sprinkled over cooked brown rice or cooked vegetables. Using gomasio as an alternative to salt is a good way of cutting back on sodium in your diet. To make it just stir 5 tablespoons of unhulled sesame seeds (the brown ones) and a level teaspoon of sea salt in a saucepan over a gentle heat until the seeds start to turn brown a smell slightly 'toasty' – this will take about 5 minutes. Transfer the mixture to an electric coffee grinder and grind to a powder. This is at its best when freshly made, but will keep well in a screw-top jar for 3–4 weeks.

Index

N

acknowledgements

Many wonderful people have helped in the production of this book, and I'd like to thank them all, starting with Jo Lal, Publisher of Nourish and Watkins, for inviting me to write it and for her support and enthusiasm throughout and my dear agent, Barbara Levy for all her help and advice. The book has been put together by a very talented team, and I'd like to thank them all: Dan Hurst, the inspiring commissioning and managing editor of Nourish; Emily Preece-Morrison, an exceptional copy editor; Georgina Hewitt for the wonderful design; Enya Todd, who supplied the lovely cover art work; Valerie Berry, who styled the food so beautifully; and Kim Lightbody, for taking such stunning photographs.

I'd like to thank, too, my wonderful friends and family, who have been so supportive and inspiring during the whole process of writing the book (which included a major house move and various upheavals – not ideal, but the way life works!). A huge thank you goes to my three exceptional daughters, Kate, Meg, and Claire, who were the subject of my earlier books on bringing up vegetarian and vegan babies and have been with me throughout my vegan journey and inspired me along the way – they have kindly given me some of their own recipes which you'll find in this book. Also my dear friend, Chryssa Porter, who has helped me so much with the testing, and re-testing of many recipes, especially the cakes; and was always there for me. Finally, and especially, to my husband, Roger, who came into my life by some miracle shortly after dear Robert died, and has been staunchly by my side throughout the process of creating, testing, and writing recipes, and survived the process!